GERMANTOWN
IN THE
CIVIL WAR

GERMANTOWN
IN THE
CIVIL WAR

EUGENE G. STACKHOUSE

With the support of the Germantown Historical Society

Charleston London

THE
History
PRESS

Published by The History Press
Charleston, SC 29403
www.historypress.net

Back cover image: The Civil War monument in Market Square in Germantown. *Courtesy of Judith Callard.*

First published 2010

Manufactured in the United States

ISBN 978.1.59629.206.2

Library of Congress Cataloging-in-Publication Data

Stackhouse, Eugene Glenn, 1939-
Germantown in the Civil War / Eugene Glenn Stackhouse.
p. cm.
Includes index.
ISBN 978-1-59629-206-2
1. Germantown (Philadelphia, Pa.)--History--19th century. 2. Philadelphia (Pa.)--History--
Civil War, 1861-1865. I. Title.
F159.G3S76 2010
974.8'1103--dc22
2010039222

Contents

Foreword

The Million Dead, Too, Summ'd Up

The dead in this war—there they lie, strewing the fields and woods and valleys and battle-fields of the south—Virginia, the Peninsula—Malvern hill and Fair Oaks—the banks of the Chickahominy—the terraces of Fredericksburgh—Antietam bridge—the grisly ravines of Manassas—the bloody promenade of the Wilderness—the varieties of the strayed dead, (the estimate of the War department is 25,000 national soldiers kill'd in battle and never buried at all, 5,000 drown'd—15,000 inhumed by strangers, or on the march in haste, in hitherto unfound localities—2,000 graves cover'd by sand and mud by Mississippi freshets, 3,000 carried away by caving-in of banks, &c.,)—Gettysburgh, the West, Southwest—Vicksburgh—Chattanooga—the trenches of Petersburgh—the numberless battles, camps, hospitals everywhere—the crop reap'd by the mighty reapers, typhoid, dysentery, inflammations—and blackest and loathesomest of all, the dead and living burial-pits, the prison-pens of Andersonville, Salisbury, Belle-Isle, &c., (not Dante's pictured hell and all its woes, its degradations, filthy torments, excell'd those prisons)—the dead, the dead, the dead—our dead—or South or North, ours all, (all, all, all, finally dear to me)—or East or West—Atlantic coast or Mississippi valley—somewhere they crawl'd to die, alone, in bushes, low gullies, or on the sides of hills—(there, in secluded spots, their skeletons, bleach'd bones, tufts of hair, buttons, fragments of clothing, are occasionally found yet)—our young men once so handsome and so joyous, taken from us—the son from the mother, the husband from the wife, the dear friend from the dear friend—the clusters of camp graves, in Georgia, the Carolinas, and in Tennessee—the single graves left in the woods or by the road-side, (hundreds, thousands, obliterated)—the corpses floated down the rivers, and caught and lodged, (dozens, scores, floated down the upper Potomac, after the cavalry engagements, the pursuit of Lee, following Gettysburgh)—some lie at the bottom of the sea—the general million, and the special cemeteries in almost all the States—the infinite dead—(the land entire saturated, perfumed with their impalpable ashes' exhalation in Nature's chemistry distill'd, and shall be so forever, in every future grain of wheat and ear of corn, and every flower that grows, and every breath we draw)—not only Northern dead leavening Southern soil—thousands, aye tens of thousands, of Southerners, crumble to-day in Northern earth.

And everywhere among these countless graves—everywhere in the many soldier Cemeteries of the Nation (there are now, I believe, over seventy of them)—as at the time in the vast trenches, the depositories of slain, Northern and Southern, after the great battles—not only where the scathing trail passed those years, but radiating since in all the peaceful quarters of the land—we see, and ages yet may see, on monuments and gravestones, singly or in masses, to thousands or tens of thousands, the significant word Unknown. (In some of the cemeteries nearly all the dead are unknown. At Salisbury, N.C., for instance, the known are only 85, while the unknown are 12,027, and 11,700 of these are buried in trenches. A national monument has been put up here, by order of Congress, to mark the spot—but what visible, material monument can ever fittingly commemorate that spot?)

Walt M. Whitman
From *Specimen Days* (1882), in *Complete Prose Works*

Preface

During the time the Civil War broke out, the population of Germantown was not very big and there were few people living in Chestnut Hill and northern Mount Airy. Historians estimate that the population of the town in 1854, when Germantown and Philadelphia consolidated, was about 6,500. By the 1860 census, it was about 7,000. It is remarkable, then, that about 2,000 people from Germantown served in the Civil War as soldiers, sailors, marines, doctors and nurses. (Of this number, five were in the Confederate army.) One street alone, Haines Street, gave so many soldiers to the war that they were known as the "Haines Street 100."

Germantown is that part of Philadelphia founded by Franz Daniel Pastorius in 1683 as the "German Township," which comprises the modern neighborhoods of Germantown, Mount Airy and Chestnut Hill. A "Germantowner" is defined in this book as anyone who lived in Germantown and/or the twenty-second ward of Philadelphia at any time in his or her life or was a member of Ellis Post Six, Grand Army of the Republic (GAR), regardless of where the member lived.

Most of the material in this book comes from contemporary nineteenth- and early twentieth-century accounts in the form of newspaper articles, obituaries and scrapbooks. The accounts have been edited for clarity. The book can only touch briefly on the many stories of Germantown and Germantowners in the Civil War. The Germantown Historical Society has much material for further study. The society is located at 5501-5503 Germantown Avenue on Market Square, Philadelphia, PA, 19144 (www. germantownhistory.org).

My research also led me to the Grand Army of the Republic Civil War Library and Museum, 4278 Griscom Street, Philadelphia, PA, 19124–3954 (garmuslib@verizon.net), in Frankford. The museum has most of the original applications for membership in Ellis Post Six, GAR, of Germantown—a very valuable resource.

All photographs are from the Germantown Historical Society archives unless otherwise indicated.

Many thanks go to Irvin Miller and Eliza Callard, for computer help, and to Judith Callard, for keeping this whole project together.

A Tribute to Naaman Keyser Ployd

Naaman Keyser Ployd was a newspaperman and Germantown historian, who was born July 20, 1840. We would have very little information on the Germantown Civil War veterans without Ployd's newspaper articles. This book would not have been possible without his work. He left us four large scrapbooks with stories and pictures of Germantown in the Civil War. He was, as well, one of the best informed men on Philadelphia history, and hundreds of his articles were published. His great-great-grandfather was Captain John Miller, who fought under George Washington in the

Naaman K. Ployd, age sixty. He was a Civil War veteran and a Germantown newspaperman and historian.

Birthplace of Naaman K. Ployd at Haines and Baynton Streets.

Ployd died in 1918 and was buried in Ivy Hill Cemetery.

Revolution. Ployd was born on East Haines Street, which was then known as Old Methodist Lane. He was a member of Company B of the 119th Pennsylvania Volunteers and was, for many years, active in the affairs of Ellis Post Six, Grand Army of the Republic, of which he was a past commander. Ployd was also a Mason and a member of the Odd Fellows. He used the pseudonyms "Mr. Mosby" and the "Man on the Corner," among others, for his newspaper articles. Ployd died April 8, 1918, at his home, 6337 Baynton Street, and is interred in Ivy Hill Cemetery.

CHAPTER 1

Beginnings

GERMANTOWN MEN AT FORT SUMTER

On April 12, 1861 at 4:30 in the morning, Confederate forces under the command of General P.G.T. Beauregard, of Lousiana, fired with artillery on the United States's Fort Sumter, which was located in the harbor of Charleston, South Carolina, beginning the Civil War. The U.S. force at Fort Sumter was the First U.S. Artillery, commanded by Major Robert Anderson.

One Germantown resident, Sergeant Charles S. Bringhurst, and one future Germantown resident, Private William Witzman [or Witzmann], were members of the First Artillery at Fort Sumter.

Bringhurst, a bricklayer by trade, enlisted on August 14, 1856, in Company E, First U.S. Artillery, and reenlisted twice during the war, serving eleven years altogether in the U.S. Army. At first he was stationed at Governors Island, New York, but he was later sent to Fortress Monroe and to Fort Dallas, Florida, near the Everglades. From there, he went to Fort Moultrie, South Carolina. He later lived at 92 East Wister Street and died in 1909.

William Witzman was born in Germany and immigrated to the United States. He enlisted on March 17, 1860, and was discharged on July 17, 1867. He was a part of the 70-man garrison at Fort Sumter when it was fired upon in April 1861.

A comrade said of him:

> *Witzman was a good, brave solider and a sterling man, and performed a daring act during the second day's light, at the time when we were expecting the fleet, which had hove into sight at the mouth of the harbor, to come to*

Charles Bringhurst, a veteran of Fort Sumter.

William Witzman, a veteran of Fort Sumter.

our assistance. Witzman and another were ordered to lower and dip our flag three times for assistance, which they did, with the shot and shell flying around them continuously.

Witzman survived the war. He lived at 174 Ashmead Street and died in 1906.

THE DEFENSE OF FORT SUMTER

By Charles S. Bringhurst

The following description of the opening of the Civil War and the firing of its first gun at Fort Sumter, was written by Charles S. Bringhurst, of Germantown. At Fort Sumter, he was a corporal in Company E, First U.S. Artillery, the defenders of the fort. Bringhurst was in the military service for many years, becoming, before his final discharge, the first sergeant of his company.

On the afternoon of December 26, 1860, Major Robert Anderson, (in command of the troops at Fort Sumter) in citizen clothes visited the city of Charleston, a short distance from Fort Sumter, and while in a hotel there overheard a conversation among a number of persons in which they stated their intention of attacking Fort Moultrie (South Carolina) in a short time. He immediately took his departure and preparations were at once made to abandon Fort Moultrie where his command, two companies of the First Artillery, were stationed.

That night after tattoo, the garrison of the fort were quietly awakened and the command given to get under arms in heavy marching order. Everything was done as silently as possible and the troops marched out to the front beach of Charleston Harbor where four boats were awaiting to convey them to their unknown destination. Oars were muffled and strict orders given to maintain silence as rebel boats were cruising in the vicinity to prevent reinforcements to the garrison.

The boats reached their journey's end, which proved to be Fort Sumter, without discovery by the rebels, although several times they came within a few feet of us and one of our boats touched the stern of a rebel tug. Landing at Fort Sumter a strong guard was posted and special precaution taken to prevent the landing of any boats, as the harbor was full. A sergeant and twelve men were detailed in Fort Moultrie to spike the guns, chop down the

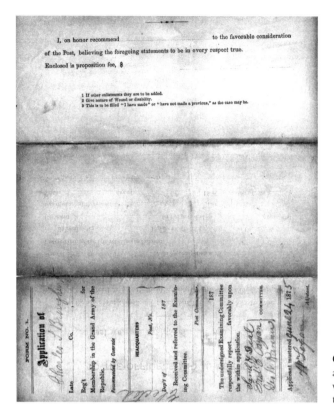

Charles Bringhurst's application after the war for membership in the GAR.

flagstaff and destroy ammunition and other material which could be used by the enemy. Early the next morning the gun-carriages were burned and the little party rejoined their command.

At reveille the American flag was raised to the breeze on Fort Sumter, the chaplain offering prayer and the band playing the "Star Spangled Banner," with the garrison forming a circle about the flag pole.

That morning the staff of the Governor of South Carolina, composed of three officers, came over to Fort Sumter from Charleston to inquire of Major Anderson his reason for evacuating Fort Moultrie and stated that they would not molest him nor "injure a hair of his head." After the return of the Governor's staff to Charleston, the South Carolinians, with State troops, took possession of Castle Pinckney and Fort Moultrie and commenced putting them in state of siege. A floating battery was built, but was found to be lopsided when it was launched.

Communication with Charleston was uninterrupted until April 11, 1861. Lieutenant Talbot, who had been dispatched from Fort Sumter to Washington and who was the bearer of return dispatches to Major Anderson, was intercepted in Charleston by Confederate authorities and was sent back to Washington without being allowed to deliver his message to Anderson. Immediately afterward the Confederates began obstructing the channel by sinking stone laden hulks and by placing patrol boats in the harbor.

On Thursday, April 11, a boat arrived at the fort bearing Colonels Chestnut and Chisholm and Captain Lee, all aides to General Beauregard. They handed Major Anderson a demand to evacuate the Fort, stating that the Confederate authorities had refrained from any act of violence, hoping that the United States Government would withdraw the troops from the fort. Major Anderson replied that he could not accept any terms of withdrawal until he heard further from his government.

Shortly after midnight, on April 12, another communication was received by Anderson from General Beauregard, desiring to know on what day Anderson would evacuate and also asking for his agreement not to open fire with his batteries unless Fort Sumter was fired upon. Major Anderson replied that he would evacuate Fort Sumter on April 15, provided that he did not receive supplies or instructions from his government. This reply was handed to Colonel Chestnut at 3 o'clock and Anderson was immediately informed that Beauregard would open fire on the fort in about one hour.

The first shell was fired from Fort Moultrie about 4:30 o'clock by a certain Samuel Ruffin of Virginia, at Ruffin's special request. The surrounding rebel batteries followed with their fire and a tremendous cannonade ensued. The Fort Sumter garrison did not open fire until daylight when they had three guns bearing on Morris Island, four on Fort Moultrie, and two on the floating battery on Sullivan's Island. The barbette guns on the parapet were soon dismounted, owing to the heavy enfilading fire of the rebels. The firing continued all day until dark. During the night Fort Sumter was silent but occasional shells were fired by the Confederates. Firing by both sides was resumed daybreak on Saturday morning, the 13th.

At about ten o'clock that morning the quarters inside the fort were set on fire by a shell from Fort Moultrie. So severe was the fire that the magazine was threatened and had to be protected by keeping wet blankets in front of the closed doors and by heaping dirt against them. Shortly after noon, Senator Wigfall, of Texas, arrived at the Fort under a white flag. Just at the time of his arrival the fort flag was shot away, but was quickly replaced upon the ramparts. On meeting Major Anderson, Senator Wigfall stated that General Beauregard wanted to know on what terms he would evacuate *the fort. Anderson adhered to his original terms, which were a salute to his own flag; removal by the garrison of camp and garrison equipage and to march out of the fort with the honors of war.*

After two visits by the aides of General Beauregard, Major Anderson's terms were accepted. During the salute to the flag on the fiftieth round the gun exploded, killing two men and injuring six. The garrison marched out of the fort with colors flying and the band playing "Yankee Doodle." The enemy supplied transportation to the fleet outside the bar and the garrison was shipped to New York on the steamer "Baltic."

During the bombardment the rebel floating battery at Sullivan's Island was silenced. The guns from Fort Sumter also compelled the abandoning of Fort Moultrie, the Confederates fearing that the magazines might be fired by the shells, some of which penetrated the walls.

JOHN ELLIS: GERMANTOWN'S FIRST CASUALTY IN THE CIVIL WAR

At the outbreak of the Civil War, our townsman, Captain Mark W. Collett, began to train some Germantown residents for service in the war. Soon after, Captain Collett became a major of the Third New Jersey Volunteers, a regiment of the First New Jersey Brigade. General Phil Kearney was its commander.

Captain Collett was followed by sixteen or more of the boys whom he had trained and who were anxious to fight. Among these Germantown residents were John Ellis and his brother, William; Luke Farley and his brother, James; James Platt; William Flue; Charles Delaney; Edward Lewis; Albert Toon; Harry Myers; John Meadows; Walter Melford; Gavin Neilson; George Hargraves; James Tatlow; and Lewis Hong. These men were mustered in Company H of that brigade.

Private John Ellis, born in 1839 in Nottingham, England, was the first casualty. He was accidentally shot on July 17, 1861, while standing sentinel at Cloud's Mills, Virginia. His death caused profound sadness throughout the camp. His body was brought home by his brother and James Platt, and his remains were interred in St. Stephen's Methodist Churchyard. (His body was moved later, about 1900, to Ivy Hill Cemetery in Philadelphia.) The whole community attended the funeral.

Ellis Post Six of the Grand Army of the Republic was named after John Ellis, and a large portrait of him stood at the center of the picture

Right: John S. Ellis, the first Germantown casualty of the Civil War.

Below: Ivy Hill Cemetery, where about 750 Civil War veterans are buried.

gallery of dead veterans in the post hall. Charles Delaney died soon after. Walter Melford was wounded at Gaines's Mill and died, as did James Farley. Luke Farley, James's brother was killed soon after. Lewis Hong fell at Cold Harbor. The commander, Colonel Mark Collett, was killed on May 3, 1863, at Salem Church, Virginia.

CHAPTER 2

The Main Germantown Units and Battles

TWENTY-SECOND REGIMENT OF PENNSYLVANIA VOLUNTEERS

First Sergeant Robert M. Bingham

Robert Bingham was an officer in one of the two Germantown companies that responded to President Abraham Lincoln's first call for troops in April 1861. He was first sergeant of Captain William B. Hubbs's company of Germantown that was mustered into service on April 23, 1861. This company had been in existence as a militia before the war, being attached to the Philadelphia Light Guard. The Germantown organization became Company F, Twenty-second Regiment of Pennsylvania Volunteers. George W. Jones, who later was a major of the 150th Pennsylvania Regiment was third sergeant of the company. After serving the three-month term of his first enlistment, Mr. Bingham again enlisted as first sergeant in Company E, 115th Pennsylvania Volunteers. He was seventy-nine years old at the time of his death in 1914. He is buried in Ivy Hill Cemetery.

TWENTY-THIRD REGIMENT OF PENNSYLVANIA VOLUNTEERS

Captain James Reeside White

Captain James Reeside White, formerly of Germantown, took a company of soldiers from Germantown to the seat of war at the breaking out of the rebellion in April 1861. He was connected at the beginning of the war with the Twenty-third Pennsylvania Volunteers, Company A. Afterward, he commanded Company H, Eighty-eighth Pennsylvania Volunteers. For many years after the war, he was in the upholstery business and was well-known to the people of Germantown. Captain White died on January 3, 1900, at the Soldiers Home in Hampton, Virginia, and was buried in the Hampton National Cemetery.

A poster urging young men to volunteer for the war effort.

150TH REGIMENT OF PENNSYLVANIA VOLUNTEERS (THE BUCKTAILS)

"Ballad of the Bucktails"

By Private Patrick Mulhatten

We are the Pennsylvania boys; from Germantown we came
  We have a noble Captain, and Jones it is his name.
  We came to meet our Country's foes—to them we ne'er would yield;
  We were bound to gain some victory or die on the battle field.
We started from Nicetown; right well I mind the day,
  Some bid their friends a last farewell and started on our way.
  We marched to Philadelphia and thinking all was right
  Till we got aboard the Harrisburg cars which took us to the fight.
We landed in Harrisburg at the closing of the day,
  When there we got refreshments to cheer us on the way.
  We next arrived in Baltimore in time to take the cars
  Which took us to the Capital of Freedom's states and stars.
From there we went to Clifburne on the old Maryland side,
  Where rolls the mild Potomac in all her former pride.
  But on that lovely hill-side we had not long to stay.
  For the brave old General Hooker soon ordered us away.
From then we went to Washington, the ship awaiting lay;
  We got on board the Fulton and went steaming on our way.
  And well I do remember how mildly blew the gale.
  When the ship was ordered for to stop, we marched to Belle Plain.
The rebels held that place once, but they ne'er will hold it more.
  In place of seven stars we planted thirty-four.
  At Chancellorsville we fought them and showed them what we could do,
  And we let them have a taste of the bucktails boys so true.
From there we went to Gettysburg our march it being so far.
  To rally around the good old flag and fight beneath its stars.
  We sent into the rebel ranks a storm of iron hail
  And we swept them from the battle field like chaff before the gale.
Our First Lieut. he fell there, we are sorry for the same,
  He was a noble young man, Chancellor was his name;
  He was a loyal young man, generous, kind and free;
  He was a credit to his country and the pride of Company B.

Henry Chancellor, killed at
the Battle of Gettysburg.

Likewise Lieutenant Keyser, I cannot pass him by,
And when we think of him, the tears fall from our eyes.
He was a noble soldier, the truth for him we'll say.
He was an honor to his parents and adorned Company A.
And to our noble Captain, a word for him we'll say.
He never likes to see his boys abused in any way.
When this cruel war is over and homeward we will go,
"And a health to Captain Jones, boys" from many a cup will flow.
When this cruel war will cease and peace return once more,
We will bid adieu to Dixie's land to seek our northern shore.
And may our sweethearts of the north to our soldiers generous be,
For we left our homes and firesides to fight for Liberty.

Private Mulhatten was a member of the 150th Pennsylvania Volunteers, Company B. He died on October 18, 1864, in Germantown from wounds received in battle.

(The poem is transcribed, with alterations in spelling and punctuation, from a manuscript in the Civil War Collections of the Library of the Germantown Historical Society. It appeared in the *Germantowne Crier* 37, no. 2.)

Lieutenant Colonel Thomas Chamberlain

Thomas Chamberlain died in March 1917 at the age of seventy-eight. He was one of the last surviving officers of the famous 150th Pennsylvania Volunteers, which was one of the Pennsylvania Bucktails commands that were recruited in Germantown. Chamberlain lived at 429 West Stafford Street in Germantown. He had been the clerk of records of the Gettysburg Battlefield Memorial Commission for five years. He was a member of Meade Post, GAR, and a companion of the Military Order of the Loyal Legion of the United States (MOLLUS) 4654.

He entered the military service on June 21, 1861, as captain of Company D, Fifth Reserves. He was severely wounded in battle a year later, and in September 1862 he was commissioned as major in the 150th Pennsylvania Volunteers. He participated in the battles of Antietam, Port Conway, Pollak's Mill, Chancellorsville and Gettysburg.

The 150th was subjected to great slaughter at Gettysburg. In that battle, Colonel Langhorne Wister, Lieutenant Colonel Henry Huidekoper, Adjutant R.L. Ashhurst and Major Chamberlain were all severely wounded in the first day's fight, and it fell upon Captain George W. Jones of Germantown to command what was left of the regiment. Of the seven hundred men in the ranks of the regiment when it entered the battle, only ninety-six reported fit for duty at night, with all the others having been killed, wounded or captured.

Thomas Chamberlain, severely wounded at Gettysburg.

The 150th Pennsylvania Volunteers, seen here at the McPherson farm, suffered heavy losses at Gettysburg.

Pickett's charge at Gettysburg.

After serving on the Rappahannock during the winter of 1863–1864, Chamberlain's health became impaired, and he resigned on March 15, 1864, with the rank of lieutenant colonel.

One account said:

> *An incident which occurred at midday on July 1st, did much to create good feelings and to stimulate the courage of the Bucktails. While waiting and watching for an enemy attack, Colonel Chamberlain's attention was called to a tall, bony man approaching from the direction of Gettysburg. The man was moving with deliberate step, carrying an Enfield rifle at "trail." He was evidently quite old and was peculiarly dressed. Fitted out in dark trousers and waistcoat, a blue swallowtail coat and high, black silk hat, he reported to Colonel Chamberlain and asked "Can I fight in your regiment?" Chamberlain referred him to Colonel Wister. "Well, old man, what do you want?" "I want a chance to fight with your regiment." "Certainly you can fight with us," said the Colonel Wister, who advised the old man to join the*

John Burns, an elderly man from Gettysburg, who asked Colonel Chamberlain if he could fight with the 150th.

line in an adjacent wood where he would be more sheltered from sun and bullets. With apparent reluctance, as if he preferred the open field, he moved towards the woods, and history has written the name of John Burns in the roll of the world's heroes, and his brave conduct is imperishably linked with the glories of Gettysburg.

Colonel Langhorne Wister

Langhorne Wister was born in Germantown, Philadelphia, on September 20, 1834. He was one of the sons of William and Sarah Logan Fisher Wister.

He received no military education, but on April 19, 1861, scarcely a week from the firing upon Fort Sumter, he entered the service. He was successful in recruiting, and when the noted Bucktail regiment was formed, he joined it and was elected captain. At Dranesville, where he first met the enemy in close combat, he stood with his company in a position where he was the object of the severest fire experienced by any of the Union troops on that field and received the warm commendations of the commander of the regiment. Two were killed and four were wounded in his single company. Six companies of the Bucktails, including Captain Wister's, were sent to join General George McClellan on the Virginia Peninsula and reached him in time to take the advance in the movement upon Mechanicsville. They were the first to meet the enemy as he came out to offer battle, and with wonderful skill and daring, they held him in check, skirmishing bravely until the main line of battle was formed behind Beaver Dam Creek and rifle pits completed. In the engagement that ensued, and in the subsequent retreat to Gaines's Mill, no troops could have acted with greater steadiness, or have rendered more efficient service.

The Bucktails were given the difficult and dangerous duty of skirmishing with the enemy while the main body fell back. In all these maneuvers and hard fighting, Captain Wister was among the most reliable and trusted in a battalion that was a special object of regard throughout the whole army. He received a severe contusion of the right ankle but was able to keep the field. And at Charles City Cross Roads, where the reserve corps for a third time in the Seven Days' fight was put at the forefront and made to bear the brunt of the battle, he suffered his part with the same unflinching valor as on the preceding fields.

Soon after the retirement of McClellan's army from the Peninsula, the formation of a Bucktail Brigade was ordered, and Captain Wister was selected to head one of the regiments—the 150th. The reputation that he had

Germantown born and bred, Langhorne
Wister continued to fight at Gettysburg even
after being hit in the jaw by a Minie ball.

gained as a leader of one of the old Bucktail companies inspired confidence
and made it from the outset almost the equal of a veteran regiment.

In the preliminary movements to the Battle of Chancellorsville, this
brigade performed a leading part, marching to Port Conway, for a feint, and
afterward operating with the First Corps to which it belonged at the lower
crossing before Fredericksburg. It finally joined the main army in the great
battle itself, occupying the right of the line and meeting every advance of the
enemy with cool courage.

At Gettysburg, Colonel Wister led his regiment upon the field at a little
before noon of the first day, where the Buford had presented a bold front
and had held the enemy in check, covering the town until the infantry
should come up. His position was upon a slight ridge, a little in rear of
that held by Buford, and in advance of Seminary Ridge. Here, exposed to
a fierce artillery fire and the frequent assaults of the enemy's infantry, he
held his men, changing front to meet every advance, until Colonel Stone,
who commanded the brigade, was badly wounded and borne from the
field, when Wister assumed control, turning over the regiment to Lieutenant
Colonel Huidekoper. The situation was becoming more and more critical,
as the enemy, having already brought up the main body of his forces, began

Langhorne Wister's grave at Laurel Hill Cemetery.

to close in on all sides and to press heavily in front. With remarkable skill, Colonel Wister maneuvered his small body of men to meet the masses brought against him until he was wounded by a Minie ball, which struck him in the face and shattered his jaw. "Colonel Wister," says Colonel Stone, in his official report, "though badly wounded in the mouth, while commanding the brigade, and unable to speak, remained in the front of the battle."

In recognition of his gallantry, General Abner Doubleday made honorable mention of him in his report and recommended him for promotion to brevet brigadier general, which was conferred by the president and confirmed by the Senate. Wister resigned his commission in February 1864 and resumed the business that he had left on entering the army—that of manufacturer of iron at Duncannon. A resolute purpose and undaunted heroism characterized him from his first entrance to military life, and the Bucktail corps had no more worthy or valiant representative. Wister was a MOLLUS 2344 member.

General Henry S. Huidekoper

Major General Henry Shippen Huidekoper, eminent soldier of the Civil War and a leader in civic life in Pennsylvania, was born on July 17, 1839, in Meadville, Pennsylvania. Upon leaving Harvard College after graduation in 1862, he gave his services to the Union and was mustered in at Harrisburg as captain of Company K, 150th Regiment of Pennsylvania Volunteers. Promotion came to him rapidly; in a short time after taking the field, he was made first lieutenant colonel and then colonel.

He particularly distinguished himself in battle. When in the hospital at Gettysburg, recovering from the loss of his right arm, he was captured by the Confederate forces and held prisoner for a short time. The loss of his arm so weakened the colonel that he was not allowed to immediately return to the field. But his patriotism chaffed at the inactivity at such a time of national stress, and he applied for any service that he might render. President Lincoln endorsed his request for service, but his health did not improve, and finally he was given an honorable discharge from the army in 1864.

Upon the conclusion of the Civil War, he was awarded the Medal of Honor "for gallantry in battle." In 1871, he was appointed brigadier general in command of the Twentieth Division of the Pennsylvania National Guard, and three years later, he was made acting major general of the Seventh Division of the Pennsylvania National Guard. Although eschewing politics,

General Henry Huidekoper lost an arm at Gettysburg. He was awarded the Medal of Honor for gallantry.

he was finally prevailed upon to accept the appointment of postmaster of Philadelphia and served for five years, taking office in 1880.

General Huidekoper was very well-known in Germantown, having resided for a number of years at the northwest corner of Cliveden and Morton Streets. Huidekoper was a MOLLUS 2934 member.

Colonel George W. Jones

At the outbreak of the Civil War, Major George W. Jones lived on Wister Street. He joined Captain William B. Hubbs's company, which was the second from Germantown to respond to President Lincoln's first call for troops; the company left Germantown on April 23, 1861, for a service of three months in the neighborhood of Baltimore. Following the three-month service, Jones was for a time attached to a Missouri regiment, and under General Sigel, he participated in the Battle of Pea Ridge, Arkansas.

In 1862, when two regiments of Pennsylvania Bucktails were organized—the 149th and the 150th—Jones recruited a company in Germantown, of which he became the captain. This was Company B of the 150th. Company A, of the same regiment, was also recruited here with C.C. Widdis as captain.

Before going to camp, Company B had its headquarters at Napfle's Hotel at Germantown Avenue and Wister Street. On September 1, Companies A,

George W. Jones of the "Bucktails."

B, E and F went into camp at Stenton, remaining until the 3rd, when they joined their regiment at Camp Curtin in Harrisburg. Colonel Langhorne Wister, of Germantown, commanded the 150th Regiment.

Jones participated in the Battles of Dabney's Mills and Chancellorsville. After the defeat at Chancellorsville, the Union army prepared to move back across the Rappahannock, and Colonel Wister detailed Jones and his company for picket duty to protect the rear while the troops crossed; Wister told the captain plainly that to safeguard the regiment it might be necessary to sacrifice Company B. The next day, Company B failed to join the regiment, and Colonel Wister sent a telegram to Germantown that the entire company had become prisoners in the hands of the Confederates. The news caused much excitement and distress among the relatives of the soldiers in Germantown, but a week later came the joyous news that the company, with not a man missing, were again in the camp of the regiment at White Oak Church. It was learned that Captain Jones and his men had escaped across the Rappahannock just as the last Union soldiers were crossing but had been unable to find their regiment for six days.

The next battle in which Jones participated, and the one in which the 150th Regiment was put to the severest test of its career, was Gettysburg. After Colonel Wister, Lieutenant Colonel H.S. Huidekoper, Adjutant Ashurst and Major Thomas Chamberlin were all severely wounded, Captain Jones, being the senior captain, then assumed command of the regiment. At night, he and Lieutenant William Kilgore, of Company A,

This is the Ninety-fifth Infantry (Gosline's Zouaves) Regimental Color. Over the winter of 1863–1864, the regiment reenlisted and was mustered out of service on July 24, 1865. Two blood-stained standards were handed in and are now in Harrisburg at the state Capitol. *Courtesy Brian Hunt and the Pennsylvania Capitol Preservation Committee.*

were the only commissioned officers fit for duty, and the latter had sustained a slight wound in the cheek. Captain Jones escaped unscathed.

In the fighting at Gettysburg, the 150th succeeded in recapturing the colors of the 149th Regiment, but shortly afterward, the 150th's color guard were mowed down. A corporal seized the flags, but soon after he was bayoneted, and the enemy then took the flags. At the end of the war, the flags were returned, and they are now in the state Capitol in Harrisburg.

In 1864, the 150th participated in the Virginia campaigns under Grant, and in February 1865, the regiment was sent to Elmira, New York, to guard prisoners. It remained there until June 23, when the men were mustered out.

On May 16, 1865, Jones was promoted to lieutenant colonel, and on June 15 of the same year, he became a colonel. It was characteristic of his modesty that, although clearly entitled to be called "colonel," he never assumed any higher title than that of "major," which he bore while in active service. The regimental flags in use at the end of the war passed into Major Jones's possession, and he retained them up to the time of his death.

Major Jones was a member of Ellis Post Six, GAR; Mitchell Lodge; Free and Accepted Masons; Philomathean Lodge; and the Independent Order of Odd Fellows.

Colonel Jones died on November 26, 1913, at age eighty, at his home at 6012 Morton Street. Interment was in Holy Sepulchre Cemetery in Cheltenham.

Major George W. Jones, later in life.

Lieutenant Charles P. Keyser

Charles P. Keyser, a descendant of the early settlers of Germantown and son of Naaman and Isabella P. Keyser, was born on October 7, 1843, in Germantown. He entered the Rittenhouse Public School when he was a lad and subsequently attended the Philadelphia High School.

At the breaking out of the rebellion, he felt that it was his duty to serve his country. With the consent of his father, he willingly left his school and his home, and, along with numerous relatives and friends, became part of the 150th Pennsylvania Regiment (Bucktails). He was at once made orderly sergeant of Company A, commanded by Captain C.C. Widdis, and he soon rose to the position of sergeant major, which he filled with marked ability. On November 14, he was commissioned second lieutenant of Company B, this being a second Germantown company and was commanded by Captain George W. Jones, who had seen service in Colonel Phelps's Missouri

Charles P. Keyser, killed on the first day of the Battle of Gettysburg.

Regiment. This famous regiment of Bucktails was an organization second to none and was destined to make a brilliant record. It was fortunate in the selection of its officers and was a regiment of harmony.

At Chancellorsville, they won glory. Then there was the hard and painful march to Gettysburg, with the regiment arriving early in the morning of July 1, 1863. Here they were met by generals Doubleday and Rowley, who reminded them that they were on their native soil. Meanwhile, shells were flying overhead from Confederate batteries beyond the ridge. The death of General Reynolds had a depressing effect and had to be avenged.

Colonel Wister, cool and collected, gave the command "Forward!" that meant death to many. Then, with colors unfurled and in full battle array, the Bucktails moved and took position on the McPherson farm. Soon they were engaged in a bloody struggle, and many fell bleeding and dying. Soon Daniels's Brigade, of North Carolina, was driven from the old railroad cut but was persistent in returning to the fray. The colors of the sister regiment (149th Pennsylvania), planted in front of the 150th Pennsylvania, proved an attraction to the enemy, who now made a desperate effort to capture them and strike the line in flank. In an instant, Colonel Wister drew his sword, calling on his gallant Bucktails to follow. Now it was a death struggle. Lieutenant Colonel Huidekoper swiftly wheeled Companies A, F and D to the left, until they were close to the enemy, who delivered a destructive fire but then gave way and fled in confusion. Two or three volleys from the 150th were poured into the retreating foe, after which Huidekoper drew back the right companies to their former position.

In this short and desperate charge, the companies named lost heavily. Unfortunately the Bucktails, like all others on this thin line, were soon overwhelmed and had to leave the bloody field covered with the dead and wounded.

Lieutenant Charles P. Keyser died on the first day of the Battle of Gettysburg.

Colonel Cornelius Comegys Widdis

Colonel Widdis was born on August 20, 1840, in Germantown. During his boyhood, he attended the Rittenhouse School and the high school of Germantown, graduating at the latter on February 14, 1856, when he was younger than sixteen years of age.

His military life with the 150th Pennsylvania Volunteers took him first to Washington, where he did guard duty with his company until early in 1863. His regiment was then transferred to the Army of the Potomac, and he was engaged in the Battle of Chancellorsville and at Gettysburg. At Gettysburg, he was wounded, and late on July 1, while in command of his regiment, he was captured. Widdis remained a prisoner until February 1865, when he was exchanged. During his captivity, he was confined at Libby Prison, Danville, Charlotte, Macon and Columbia.

Widdis was wounded and captured at Gettysburg.

He was one of the six hundred officers placed in Charleston for purpose of preventing the government from firing into that city. Twice while a prisoner he escaped and was retaken.

Colonel Widdis was a member of MOLLUS (4177).

114ᵀᴴ Pennsylvania Regimental Band (Collis's Zouaves)

Private Edward W. Campion

Charles H.T. Collis, of Philadelphia, organized a regiment of Zouaves in 1862, which was enlisted as the 114ᵗʰ Pennsylvania Volunteers. While being recruited, the regiment was encamped in the lower part of Germantown. A few years before that, the National Cornet Band had been organized in Germantown. The members were all young men just taking up the study of music. Captain F.A. Elliott, who was in the wool business, was very interested in the band, supplying them with instruments and otherwise helping them. At his suggestion, the band joined Collis's Zouaves, with all the members enlisting on August 11, 1862. Edward Campion played a horn in the band. On August 29, the band left Philadelphia with the regiment to join the Army

Edward W. Campion was a member of the 114th Pennsylvania Regimental Band during the war.

of the Potomac. In the early days of the war, every regiment took along a band. Congress decided to allow but one band to each brigade. The Zouave Band was retained, and for a time, it was the only band of an entire division.

The band consisted of fifteen members, and it remained intact during the three years of service. In times of battle, the members of the band gave valuable help to the surgeons in caring for the wounded. In 1883, during the dedication of the soldiers' monument in Market Square, the survivors of the band marched in line once more, playing wartime melodies that had often cheered the soldiers on the march through the Southern states. General Collis was present at the dedication, and when the band appeared, he shouted: "Give us 'Hell on the Rappahannock.'" This was a startling selection because of its noisy features and had been a favorite among Collis's men. Complying with the general's request, the band played it, and the bass drum, the cymbals and the big horn did their duty in a way that delighted the old soldiers.

The uniform consisted of red trousers, Zouave jacket, white leggings, blue sash and white turban. The material for the uniforms was imported from France, and a sufficient supply was obtained to replenish the uniforms when they were worn out. Thus, the regiment continued to wear the Zouave uniform until the end of its service.

Collis's Zouaves, in their distinctive uniforms, were the 114th Regimental Band. Besides playing in the band, the members assisted with nursing duties.

Musician Frank Rauscher

"The Capture of the Germantown Band at Fredericksburg"

Published in the Germantown Independent-Gazette, *November 14, 1902*

By Frank Rauscher

When in 1861 President Lincoln called for 300,000 additional men to suppress the rebellion, Col. C.H.T. Collis was authorized to raise the One Hundred and Fourteenth Regiment. He determined that the uniforms should be that of the original Zouaves d'Africque. It was the only regiment that held to the Zouave uniform until the close of the war. The lamented Captain F.A. Elliott, of Germantown, raised Company F, of the new command. The officers of the regiment determined to take a band with them and called upon the leader of the Germantown Band, who presented the matter to the members, all of whom, with one or two exceptions, volunteered their services. As soon as organized the regiment was called to Washington, the rebels at that time being en route for Antietam, where a battle was subsequently fought. The 114th Regiment joined the Army of the Potomac, and were united with the Third Corps.

At Fredericksburg, the first battle in which they participated, they were placed on the left of the line. When Meade with his Pennsylvania reserves attacked the rebel lines and drove them back some distance, and was in turn attacked by the reinforced Confederates and sharply pushed, being compelled to call for assistance, the Third Corps was thrown across the pontoon in his support. The band kept its position at the head of the regiment until the shot and shell fell thick and fast around, when they were ordered to the rear, where, in company with the surgeons, they established the field hospital. Soon the wounded began to arrive, and our constant attention all that day and night was required in their care.

The following day, there being a lull in the fighting, the Division Commander, General Birney, called on the band for music. After obliging with several patriotic airs, it retired for the night, a spot being selected about one hundred yards in the rear of the line of battle. The position was in a sort of small ravine or ditch, not unlike an old railroad cut, where in case of a renewal of battle it would be safe. Being worn out from loss of sleep, on the previous night, and it being dismal and rainy, the boys of the band covered themselves with their rubber blankets and were soon wrapped in peaceful slumber.

Early in the morning the leader started out, in company with his brother, in search of wood with which to boil the coffee. In going along the ravine they were surprised to see canteens and other utensils scattered about, as if hastily abandoned, but never suspected the real state of affairs. They had not proceeded far when they were met by a mounted officer, in rubber coat, who accosted them, asking what they were doing there. They gave him to understand that they were members of the band. He than informed them that they were his prisoners. The leader, of course, still taking the stranger for a Union officer, told him he understood his duty. The officer smilingly opened his rubber coat at this point and displayed his grey uniform, remarking, "Come up here and I'll show you how your army has left you. It is now on the other side of the Rappahannock. The pontoons are up, our line is between you and the river, and you are prisoners."

The information was somewhat startling, but, unfortunately, proved too true, for on mounting the bank they saw the whole rebel line, cheering *lustily, while along the river front a strong skirmish line had been posted. The members of the band, as soon as they had recovered from the surprise, packed up their traps and marched into the rebel lines, and were taken to General Archer's headquarters. They were ordered to pile their instruments in a heap. General Archer remarked as they did, "I just wanted a new set for our band." The leader, of course, remonstrated at the wholesale confiscation, and informed the rebel officer that the instruments were private property. "Confound you," said Archer, "you Yankees captured me once, and you took a $2,000 horse of mine and everything I had and that was all private property, too." Regretfully the instruments were parted with.*

The manner in which the band came to be bottled up was this. Our army had retreated during the night, very hastily and quietly, strict orders being given not even to rattle the canteens. The pontoons had been covered with straw to deaden the sound as they passed over. The division to which the band was attached passed right and left within a few yards of its bivouac, never thinking for a moment it was leaving it. The doctors who were within a few yards of the musicians escaped, moving off without notifying the latter. Most of the captured in the battle, about 400 in all (outside of the wounded), left in that ravine as were the musicians during the retreat, were non-combatants. The band was sadly missed by the regiment, as it had greatly improved and its members were general favorites. The day it was captured its members were taken to Stonewall Jackson's headquarters and paroled. They were sent thence to Richmond, but did not succeed in seeing the "bright" side of Libby Prison, where they remained for five weeks, until they were sent for by the United States flag of truce boat.

The band afterwards had the pleasure of seeing the rebel General Archer, who had made them hand over their instruments so summarily a prisoner in the Union hands, he having been captured at the Battle of Gettysburg, the first day of the fight, by the First Army Corps.

Frank Rauscher was a native of Alsace-Lorraine, having been born on October 8, 1832, at Saverne. He came to Philadelphia in 1850. He died on August 28, 1903, in his seventy-first year. The funeral services were held at his residence at 330 West School House Lane. He was buried in Ivy Hill Cemetery. His experiences and recollections of the Army of the Potomac, from 1862 to 1865, were interestingly recorded in a book, *Music on the March*, published around 1893.

CHAPTER 3

The Lost and We Who Remain

Germantown's Veterans

These are only a few of the Germantown veterans who served in the Civil War. The accounts come from a variety of sources—Naaman Ployd's scrapbooks, obituaries and newspaper articles—and have been edited for clarity.

CANNONEER FREDERICK W. BENDER

Frederick Bender was a Frenchman by birth and a man of a most engaging personality. Besides being a hero of the Civil War, he fought in the French Revolution of 1848 and the Franco-Prussian War, and at the time of his death, he carried with him several scars from wounds he received. He was a cannoneer in the French artillery, stationed in Paris when King Louis Philippe was dethroned and driven into exile. General Cavignac, commander in chief of the army, was made dictator, and when the infuriated populace fired on the soldiers Cannoneer Bender was wounded by a bullet striking him in the leg.

When the Civil War broke out, Cannoneer Bender—like many others in the French army—resigned, came to this country and enlisted on the Union side. He first served in the Second Pennsylvania Volunteers, and the U.S. government, learning he was an experienced gunner, induced him to accept service on the gunboat *Princeton*. From this vessel, he was transferred to the sloop of war *Tuscarora* as a gunner. He was with Admiral David Farragut at the passing of Fort Morgan; he joined in the storming of Fort Fisher, where he was wounded; and he was in many other important naval engagements.

When the Franco-Prussian War was declared, Mr. Bender went back to his native land and joined the artillery corps. He had charge of a gun at the Battle of Gravelotte, where the German cavalry, under the command of General Steinmetz, were frightfully slaughtered while attempting to break the French lines. Bender was in Paris when the red flag, the symbol of anarchistic freedom, held sway and the Tuileries were converted into hospitals. When the war ended, he returned to the United States. Mr. Bender was often heard to declare that the American soldier has no equal as a fighter.

Frederick W. Bender died on April 4, 1906, at age seventy-three. His funeral took place at his residence at 14 Maplewood Avenue. Services were held at St. Vincent de Paul's Church on East Price Street, and interment was at Holy Sepulchre Cemetery in Cheltenham.

FIRST LIEUTENANT HILLARY BEYER

Hillary Beyer was born on September 28, 1837, near Norristown. When the Civil War broke out, he enlisted in Company A, Ninetieth Regiment, Pennsylvania Volunteers, and served with distinction throughout the conflict. He was injured on May 5, 1864, at the Battle of the Wilderness, but he was never off duty. At the Battle of Antietam, Beyer, who had risen to the rank of lieutenant, performed an act of gallantry that the records of the many brave deeds of the war show nothing more heroic. For his conspicuous courage on this occasion, Congress awarded him the Medal of Honor. One of the acts of personal bravery and self-sacrifice made by Lieutenant Beyer was when he remained out on the open battlefield at Antietam, carried one of the wounded men, James H. Gouldy, some distance to the rear of the line of battle and placed him behind a rock, giving the wounded man protection from the enemy's bullets. At the time, he was subjected to a very heavy artillery and infantry fire from the enemy.

Beyer's death occurred on September 24, 1907. His funeral took place at his residence at 69 East Clapier Street. He was buried in the Presbyterian Church Yard, Lower Providence, in Montgomery County, Pennsylvania.

COLONEL ALEXANDER BIDDLE

Colonel Alexander Biddle was born on April 29, 1819, in Philadelphia and was the son of Thomas Biddle, head of the old banking firm of Thomas Biddle and Company, and grandson of Clement Biddle, quartermaster general under Washington. His maternal grandfather was General Jonathan Williams, an engineer in the United States Army and the organizer and first superintendent of the West Point Military Academy. Biddle graduated from the University of Pennsylvania and afterward entered the counting house of Bevan & Humphries, the largest shipping firm in Philadelphia at that time. He was absent for two years, and upon returning home, he entered his father's firm and devoted himself to the banking business until the outbreak of the Civil War, when he was chosen as major of the Twenty-first Pennsylvania Volunteers.

He participated with his regiment in the Battles of Fredericksburg, Chancellorsville and Gettysburg, winning his promotion of lieutenant colonel by splendid conduct and exhibitions of bravery. After eighteen months' service, he returned home and withdrew from private business, instead engaging in public enterprises. In 1874, he was elected a member of the board of directors of the Pennsylvania Railroad. He was a director of the Pennsylvania Company for Insurances on Lives and Granting Annuities, the Dime Savings Fund Society, the Contributionship Insurance Company, the Lehigh Coal and Navigation Company and quite a number of smaller institutions of good financial repute. Upon the reorganization of the Board of City Trusts, he was made a member, and in January 1882, Biddle was its president. In 1868, Biddle was made a member of the board of managers of the Pennsylvania Hospital and was reelected annually for many years. Mr. Biddle always took a deep interest in the affairs of Girard College and was quite prominent in its management. He was a vestryman of St. Paul's Protestant Episcopal Church, Chestnut Hill and a member of MOLLUS (6248).

Colonel Biddle died on May 2, 1899, at his Chestnut Hill residence on the Bethlehem Pike. He was buried in Laurel Hill Cemetery.

PRIVATE DANIEL W. BUSSINGER

Daniel Bussinger was born at the Falls of the Schuylkill in 1843. When he was seven years of age, he was admitted to Girard College, where he remained for eight years; in 1858, he became an apprentice to a farmer in Washington County, Pennsylvania, where he lived for three years. In August 1861, he ran away and enlisted as a volunteer in the United States Army, but he was brought back by his guardian. In December of the same year, he reenlisted in the Tenth Regiment of the Pennsylvania Reserve Volunteer

Later in life, Daniel W.
Bussinger became warden of
Eastern State Penitentiary.

Corps. He served as a private and then reenlisted for the war as a veteran. While on picket duty, he was taken prisoner at Spotsylvania Courthouse and incarcerated in Libby Prison. After a stay of three weeks, he was sent with other prisoners to the famous Andersonville Stockade Prison. He went later to Savannah, Georgia, and other places, returning from the war to Germantown, where he secured employment at the carpet mills of McCallum, Crease & Sloan. He eventually received an appointment in the custom house, and two years later, he was appointed to a clerkship. Here he remained for six years until 1877, when he was promoted to a clerkship in the Eastern Penitentiary and finally warden of the institution. Few men took a more active interest in the Grand Army of the Republic than Bussinger, having been a charter member of Ellis Post Six and filling important positions of trustee, representative and commander.

"Dan" Bussinger died on January 13, 1931, at the Roxborough Memorial Hospital at age eighty-eight.

CORPORAL JAMES BOISBRUN

At the beginning of the war, Corporal James Boisbrun enlisted for three months' service in the 23rd Pennsylvania Volunteers, Company F, and upon the expiration of that term, he entered the 110th Pennsylvania Volunteers, under Colonel Frank Patterson. He remained with this regiment until the close of the war. Namaan K. Ployd, a longtime close friend of Mr. Boisbrun and one of the hundred or more men who enlisted from Haines Street wrote thus about his comrade: "Corporal Jim was one of the first to respond to President Lincoln's call for troops to defend the Union and one of the last to leave the service after the war was over and the Union saved."

At the Battle of Chancellorsville, Virginia, a Confederate bullet entered his body, and he was sent to the army hospital at Germantown for treatment. There, notwithstanding his dangerous wound, he acted as nurse to the wounded comrades and was a useful man to the surgeons.

James Boisbrun, one of the "Haines Street Hundred" who enrolled to fight.

Boisbrun was born in a house at Germantown Avenue and School House Lane, which is now the site of a bank.

He was made orderly and bearer of dispatches for Major General Mott. Among the hundreds of dispatches carried by Corporal Boisbrun, often through the enemy's country, was one announcing the fall of Richmond and another announcing the assassination of President Lincoln.

Mr. Boisbrun was born on August 31, 1827, in an old building that stood at Germantown Avenue and School Lane. His father was Stephen Boisbrun, who conducted a store there. He died on December 11, 1910. Interment was at Northwood Cemetery. Ellis Post Six, GAR, of which Mr. Boisbrun had been a member for many years, attended the funeral.

LIEUTENANT COLONEL EMLEN NEWBOLD CARPENTER

Emlen N. Carpenter served with the First City Troop in the three months' campaign, and in September of 1861, he joined the Sixth Pennsylvania Cavalry, Rush's Lancers, as second lieutenant of Company D, being promoted soon after to first lieutenant. He acted as special aide to General Franklin at Fredericksburg; after rejoining his command, Carpenter was promoted captain of Company E, which formed as part of Captain Starr's squadron as bodyguard to General Hooker, who was then commanding the army of the Potomac. In this capacity, Carpenter served at Chancellorsville.

Subsequently, he accompanied Captain Starr and a small body of men to carry dispatches from Hooker at Fairfax Courthouse to General Alfred Pleasanton, at Aldie, Virginia, and served on the staff of the latter in the engagement of June 18. At Gettysburg, he was on General George Meade's staff. He was taken prisoner in the fight at Todd's Tavern and sent to Libby Prison, then to Macon, Georgia. There he met his brother, John Quincy Carpenter, an officer of the 150th Pennsylvania, of the Bucktail Brigade, First Army Corps; John was captured at the first day's fight at Gettysburg and had been a prisoner since that time.

About the end of July 1864, Captain Carpenter was shipped by rail for Charlotte, but before reaching that place, he jumped from the car and made his escape to within five miles of the Union lines, when he was recaptured. He was then taken to Charleston and confined in the jail. After three weeks of terrible suffering, he was removed to the hospital, but when yellow fever broke out among the prisoners in October 1864 they were shipped to Columbia. When they were near Orangeburg, Carpenter, this time accompanied by his brother, again escaped by jumping from the train and set out for east Tennessee.

After many trials, they were recaptured in a swamp and taken to Columbia, where the prisoners were confined in the enclosure of the insane asylum. Hearing of the approach of General William T. Sherman, Carpenter and a few others tried one more effort to escape. By means of a knife, they succeeded in cutting holes into the ceiling of a wooden building in the yard, and when the prisoners were removed, they concealed themselves between the ceiling and the roof. They were driven from this retreat when the buildings were fired upon the departure of the Confederates. Carpenter was befriended by a lady in the town, who concealed him in her cellar, and the next morning before light, a Negro took him to an empty outhouse, from where he soon beheld the sight of Sherman's advancing column; his deliverance was at last achieved. Recognized by a friend on Sherman's staff, Carpenter was ordered to report to General Howard, who at once took him into his military family as an aide. Reequipped after his long privations, he served with Howard through the Carolina campaign and until the entry into Fayetteville, when he obtained leave of absence to visit his family, who had heard nothing of him for more than a year and a half.

Carpenter died in 1891 at his home on the estate of his father, the late George W. Carpenter, at Germantown Avenue and Carpenter Lane. He was buried in the family vault at St. Luke's Church. He had been a member of MOLLUS (3398).

Michael Cody (or Coady) was a seaman on the USS *Lancaster*.

SEAMAN MICHAEL J. COADY

Michael J. Coady enlisted in 1864 as a seaman on the USS *Lancaster*. He was on a ship that sank the Confederate *Ram Albemarle*. After the war, he became a member of the Philadelphia Fire Department. He lived at 856 East Woodlawn Street.

CAPTAIN FRANCIS A. DONALDSON

Captain Francis A. Donaldson served with the 188th Pennsylvania, Corn Exchange Regiment, and was a member of MOLLUS (2072). He was a descendant of Hans and Jane de Neus, founders of Nicetown.

Captain Francis
Adams Donaldson.

CAPTAIN FRANK A. ELLIOTT

Germantown's citizens were surprised when, in the summer of 1862, Frank A. Elliott, a wealthy resident of the place and whose life had always been quiet and unostentatious, began to recruit a company of soldiers for service in the Civil War. He was a native of Massachusetts but had lived in Germantown for some years; his home was on Price Street near Baynton. He was engaged in the wool business in Philadelphia.

The company that he organized and of which he was made captain became Company F, of the 114th Pennsylvania Volunteers, known as Collis's Zouaves. It was largely through Captain Elliott that the old Germantown

51

Cornet Band became the band of the regiment. An appropriation of six hundred dollars from city council was devoted to equipping the band.

Captain Elliott served with his company until May 3, 1863, when he lost his life in the Battle of Chancellorsville. His body was never recovered.

PRIVATE MELLVILLE H. FREAS

Private Mellville H. Freas was born on January 26, 1841, and was a well-known character in Germantown; he lived most of his life in Germantown and died at 428 East Haines Street, within two blocks of the house in which he was born. To the local children, he was affectionately known during the latter years of his life as "Grandpop" and "Santa Claus."

He enlisted in Company A, 150th Pennsylvania Volunteers, at the outbreak of the Civil War. He was taken prisoner at the Battle of Gettysburg on July 1, 1863, with four other boys from Germantown: Louis Vogle, Phillip Hammer, Charles Grant and George Shingle. He was confined at Andersonville until the end of the war.

After the war ended, Mr. Freas was a letter carrier and subsequently became an auctioneer. He was a member of Ellis Post Six, GAR, and attended the Methodist church.

He died on January 22, 1920. Mr. Freas was survived by two daughters, Mrs. Charles Matheson and Mrs. Laura M. Johnson; fourteen grandchildren; and seven great-grandchildren. Funeral services were held in the chapel of Kirk & Nice in Germantown, followed by interment in Ivy Hill Cemetery.

"Orders His Own Statue to be Placed in Cemetery: Civil War Veteran Prepares for Death"

Newspaper article, 1907

Mellville H. Freas, a Civil War Veteran and a former member of the famous Bucktail Regiment yesterday awarded a contract to John W. Gessler's Sons, 39th street and Baltimore Avenue, to make a granite statue of him which will be placed in his lot in Ivy Hill Cemetery.

It was in Germantown that with four companions he enlisted in 1862 in the 150th Pennsylvania Volunteers, known as the Bucktails. The five young men remained together until Gettysburg. At 6 o'clock on July 3, 1863, as General Lee was preparing for flight, they were captured. They

Mellville Freas's statue in Ivy Hill Cemetery.

were taken to the prison at Belle Isle, where Freas's four companions died.

At the close of the war he returned to Germantown, and erected a monument upon his lot In Ivy Hill, on which were cut the names of the four friends he lost in prison. Every Memorial Day since then Freas has donned his uniform and has gone to the cemetery to decorate the monument.

The monument has the following inscription:

MELLVILLE H. FREAS,

A Soldier of the Civil War

1862–1865

Company A, 150ᵗʰ Pa. Vols. The Bucktail Regiment

Taken prisoner at Gettysburg July 3, 1863 at 6 p.m. Was in prison at Belle Isle, Va. Paroled March 4 1864.

PRIVATE ALFRED C. GIBSON

Private Alfred C. Gibson, believed to have been the last-surviving official of the court that tried the conspirators in President Lincoln's assassination, died in February 1931 at his home at 19 West Phil-Ellena St. He was eighty-one. Gibson was clerk to General John F. Hartranft, who was commander of the military prison at Washington where the conspirators who plotted with John Wilkes Booth were imprisoned, tried and executed. Gibson was attached to the 215th Pennsylvania Regiment, Company D.

SURGEON HENRY ERNEST GOODMAN

Dr. Henry Ernest Goodman, one of the six sons of Henry Goodman and Maria Earnest Goodman, graduated from the medical department of the University of Pennsylvania in 1859. After graduation, he was appointed a resident physician to the Philadelphia Hospital; upon completing his term,

The Goodman family gravestone in Trinity Lutheran Churchyard.

he received an appointment as resident physician to the Wills Eye Hospital, where he became interested in the specialty to which he devoted the greater part of his time after the war.

On July 23, 1861, he was made major and surgeon of the 28th Pennsylvania Infantry, discharged for appointment in the United States Volunteers on April 19, 1864. He also became first lieutenant and assistant surgeon in the United States Volunteers on February 26, 1864; major and surgeon, May 18, 1864; lieutenant colonel and medical director, United States Volunteers (by assignment), February 25, 1865 to April 1, 1865; colonel and medical director, United States Volunteers (by assignment), April 2, 1865, to June 10, 1865; and brevetted lieutenant colonel and colonel, United States Volunteers, March 13, 1865, "for faithful and meritorious services during the war." Goodman then resigned and was honorably discharged on November 3, 1865.

He was a member of the Grand Army of the Republic, Army of the Cumberland, Army of the Potomac and the Army of Georgia. He was also a member of MOLLUS 201.

In 1866, he received the appointment as United States examining surgeon for pensions. From 1866 to 1873, he was the port physician at Philadelphia. He was appointed by Mayor Warwick as a member of the Board of Civil Service Examiners. Dr. Goodman was one of the founders and surgeons of the Orthopaedic Hospital and Infirmary for Nervous Diseases and the secretary of the medical staff, a position he held until his death. He was also one of the founders of the Maternity Hospital and the consulting surgeon.

In 1874, Dr. Goodman married the widow of John White Geary, a former Pennsylvania governor. On February 3, 1896, Dr. Goodman ran for a train at Tioga Station, and when he reached it, he fell dead on the platform of one of the cars. Dr. Goodman was buried in the churchyard of Trinity Lutheran Church in Germantown, a church where his brother-in-law was pastor for fifty years.

COLONEL SAMUEL GOODMAN

Colonel Samuel Goodman served throughout the Civil War. He was made second lieutenant of the 28th Pennsylvania Infantry on October 15, 1861, and first lieutenant and adjutant on November 13, 1861. He was honorably mustered out on August 1864. Over the years of his service Goodman was named brevetted captain, major, lieutenant colonel and colonel for gallant

Left: Samuel Goodman Jr. in uniform.

Below: Samuel Goodman's house in Chestnut Hill.

and meritorious service at the Battles of Cedar Mountain, Antietam, Chancellorsville, Gettysburg, Lookout Mountain, Mission Ridge, Ringgold, Mill Creek Gap and Resaca. He was awarded the Medal of Honor for saving the colors of the 107th Ohio Volunteers at the Battle of Chancellorsville. Goodman was also a member of MOLLUS (1037).

Goodman, a former councilman from the Twenty-second Ward and a prominent businessman, died on March 23, 1914, at Palm Beach, Florida, from dropsy. He was seventy-five years old. His home was at Germantown and Chestnut Hill Avenues in Chestnut Hill. He was a member of the Union League and of the Philadelphia Cricket Club. He was interred in the Trinity Lutheran Churchyard.

COLONEL ALEXANDER L. HAWKINS

Colonel Alexander L. Hawkins, late commander of the Tenth Pennsylvania Volunteers, died at sea while returning from the Philippines. He served as a private in the Civil War until after the Battle of Chickamauga in the famous Fifteenth Pennsylvania Cavalry, which included the following Germantowners: David C. King, John O. Stokes, Howard A. Buzby, Henry Hergesheimer, William Benner, Abram Thomas, Charles Garver, William Johnson, William Topham and Jacob Henvis.

LIEUTENANT JOHN STORY JENKS

Lieutenant John Story Jenks was born on October 29, 1839, near Baltimore, the son of William Pearson Jenks and Elizabeth Story Jenks. He was educated in the public schools of Philadelphia, including Central High School, from which he was graduated in February 1856. In 1862, Jenks enlisted in the army and was made a second lieutenant of Company L, Seventh Regiment, Pennsylvania Militia. In 1883, he was made first lieutenant of Battery L, Thirty-second Regiment and was a member of the Veteran Corps of that regiment.

He was a philanthropist and former member of the board of education. He belonged to the Union League, the City Club and the Penn Club. He was a member of the Historical Society of Pennsylvania, the Numismatic and Antiquarian Society and the Colonial Society.

Jenks died in 1923. Funeral services were held at his home at 154 Bethlehem Pike. A public school in Chestnut Hill is named for Lieutenant Jenks.

CAPTAIN JULIUS A. KAISER

Captain Julius A. Kaiser, a Civil War veteran, lived at 508 Locust Avenue in Germantown (now the home of this book's author). Kaiser was married to a member of the Bringhurst family and was a well-known chess champion. A fellow naval officer, Dr. E. Stanley Perkins, came to live in the house because of illness. He died there in May 1901. Captain Kaiser died in January 1915. He was buried in West Laurel Hill Cemetery. He had been a member of MOLLUS (3091).

Above: 508 East Locust Avenue, where Captain Julius Kaiser and Dr. E. Stanley Perkins lived at the end of their lives.

Left: Captain Julius Kaiser.

John Krause, Eleventh
Pennsylvania Volunteers,
Company D.

John J. Krause

John J. Krause, a member of Eleventh Pennsylvania, Company D, was listed as being a prisoner at Andersonville. He is buried at Zion Evangelical Lutheran Burial Ground.

Major William Harrison Lambert

Major William H. Lambert, Civil War veteran, financier and author died in June 1912. His funeral was held at his residence at 330 West Johnson Street. Services were conducted by his pastor, the Reverend John Harvey Lee of the Second Presbyterian Church, and many men prominent in church, financial and military circles were present. The honorary pallbearers were ex-governor Edwin Stuart, General Louis Wagner and Messrs. John T. Nicholson, William Potter, John Story Jenks, John D. McIlhenny, Richard Dale Sparhawk and Samuel Y. Heebner. Major Lambert was interred in West Laurel Hill Cemetery.

Medal of Honor winner William H. Lambert became known for his collection of Lincolniana.

Lambert, a member of the Fifteenth Pennsylvania Cavalry and MOLLUS (1985), had a brilliant war record. He was brevetted major on March 13, 1865, and received the Medal of Honor. Lambert was president of the State Department of Charities and Correction from 1892 to 1899. For many years, he was a member of the Union League. He was made a director of that organization in 1901 and served until 1904; in 1903 and 1904, he was secretary. He was a member of Post Two, GAR, and the Historical Society of Pennsylvania.

He was the author of *Lincoln Literature*, *The Faith of Abraham Lincoln* and several other works. He had a valuable collection of Lincoln and Thackeray mementoes and also many valuable relics of the Civil War. A newspaper article, "Lambert's Lincolniana," noted that Lambert's collection would be given to the Lincoln Museum in Springfield, Illinois, the home of the emancipator.

CAPTAIN HENRY D. LANDIS

Military matters had always a lively interest for Captain Henry D. Landis, and during the war, he rendered good service to the Union as the captain of Landis's Battery. In 1865, Landis enlisted as a private in Company C, 215th

Pennsylvania Volunteers and served until the regiment was mustered out on July 31, 1865. Landis, a well-known hardware merchant, died on February 1895, at age seventy-one. He left a widow, two daughters and three sons, one of whom, R.F. Landis, was a cavalry lieutenant in the regular army. Captain Landis was interred in Lancaster Cemetery in Lancaster, Pennsylvania.

PRIVATE JACOB LIPP

Private Jacob H. Lipp was born on December 23, 1839, in Germany and came to Germantown at the age of twelve. He was a veteran of the Civil War, having been connected for four years with the U.S. Marine Corps. He was captured by Captain Raphael Semmes, a Confederate naval captain, whose ship, the *Alabama*, terrorized U.S. shipping during the war.

He was a past commander of Ellis Post Six, and he was one of the oldest members of Germantown Lodge, Knights of Pythias and Walker Lodge of Odd Fellows. He was a member of the board of directors of the Germantown Business Men's Association.

He died at age seventy-two at his home at 28 West Haines Street. He was interred at Ivy Hill Cemetery.

Private Jacob Lipp was in the U.S. Marine Corps.

PRIVATE JOHN E. MANSHIP

Private John E. Manship, Fifth Pennsylvania Cavalry.

Private John E. Manship lived at 5839 Morton Street for about a half century. He was born in 1848 in Leicester, England, and was brought to America when he was an infant. In 1864, when he was only sixteen years old, Manship enlisted in Company B, Fifth Pennsylvania Cavalry, and served in that command until the end of the war.

Manship was a member of Ellis Post Six beginning in 1879, and for some years he was librarian of the post. He was also a member of the committee in charge of the memorial tablets at Market Square. He died on February 22, 1913, at age sixty-four. Interment was made in Ivy Hill Cemetery.

PRIVATE NATHAN MARPLE

Private Nathan Marple was the youngest of three brothers, the others being John and Amos, who all served in the Civil War. They lived on West Rittenhouse Street at the time of the war. The two elder brothers joined Colonel Rush's Sixth Pennsylvania Cavalry; when young Nathan also presented himself for enlistment, he was told to go home and "report to his mother," being declared too young. He did as directed, but subsequently he was accepted in the Third New Jersey Cavalry.

He died in May 1922 at age seventy-six.

Private Isaac R. Martindell

Private Isaac R. Martindell died on April 28, 1898. He lost his left foot at the Battle of Gettysburg.

A large number of friends, also members of Ellis Post Six, GAR, the 150th Regiment Pennsylvania Volunteers (Bucktails), the Maimed Soldiers' Pension League and the employees of the Bureau of Highways, attended the funeral services at his residence at 66 West Washington Lane. Interment was at Ivy Hill Cemetery.

Masland Family

Second Lieutenant Alfred Masland

Second Lieutenant Alfred Masland, a weaver by trade, was born in England and came to Germantown with his wife in 1837. When the war broke out, he enlisted in Company B, Third Regiment, New Jersey Volunteers. He was discharged on April 11, 1863, on account of a number of wounds; reenlisted on January 4, 1864, in Company B, Second Regiment, Pennsylvania Heavy Artillery; and was promoted to the position of second lieutenant.

He died on March 16, 1895, at St. Timothy's Hospital in Roxborough; the funeral took place at the residence of his nephew, Joseph H. Masland of 17 Mechlin Street. Second Lieutenant Masland was a member of Ellis Post Six, GAR. He was buried in Ivy Hill Cemetery.

Private Charles Henry Masland

Private Charles Henry Masland was born in Germantown on December 15, 1841, and lived at 1224 Sixty-ninth Avenue in Oak Lane. He first enlisted on April 21, 1861, in the Twenty-third Pennsylvania Volunteers and was discharged September 1, 1861, in Philadelphia. Masland reenlisted on September 17, 1861, with Company E, Sixth Pennsylvania Cavalry, and was discharged on September 17, 1864, at Harpers Ferry.

He died March 26, 1934, and was buried in Ivy Hill Cemetery.

Sergeant James William Masland

Sergeant James William Masland was born on August 13, 1840, in Germantown and died on April 19, 1924, in Bucks County, Pennsylvania. Masland served in the Twenty-third Pennsylvania Regiment, Company F.

He was buried in Ivy Hill Cemetery.

Sergeant John Thurmand Masland

Sergeant John Thurmand Masland was born on August 4, 1817, in Nottingham, England, and died on January 3, 1883, in Germantown. He served in the Seventy-first Pennsylvania Regiment, Company E.

The family founded James W. Masland & Co., a carpet manufacturer of Kensington.

Major Matthew Henry Masland

Major Matthew Henry Masland was born on November 30, 1821, and died on February 27, 1872. He served in the Second Pennsylvania Heavy Artillery Regiment.

CORPORAL ALEXANDER MATHUES

Corporal Alexander Mathues was born on July 2, 1835, of revolutionary stock. His grandfather, William Mathues, passed through Germantown with Washington during the war with Great Britain, and his father, William Mathues, fought in the War of 1812. Corporal Mathues enlisted in the Union army in 1861, and by 1863, he had attained the rank of corporal. In that year, he was wounded over the heart by a piece of shell and was taken to the hospital on David Island.

Mathues died on July 25, 1907, at the residence of his son-in-law, William W. Weissman of 21 Schoolhouse Lane. Interment was at Ivy Hill Cemetery.

First Lieutenant John B. Maxwell

First Lieutenant John B. Maxwell was a corporal in the second company that went to the war from Germantown. That was a company of the Pennsylvania Light Guard that had been in existence for some years prior to the war; its meeting place was in Langstrom's Hall at Germantown and Chelten Avenues. The company responded to Lincoln's first call for troops and left Germantown on April 23, 1861, under the command of Captain W.B. Hubbs. It became Company F, Twenty-second Pennsylvania Regiment. After the expiration of the three months' term of service, Maxwell helped to organize Company I, Ninety-fifth Pennsylvania Volunteers, of which he became first lieutenant. He served nineteen months with this company.

After the war, Maxwell was proprietor of the General Wayne Hotel, located at Germantown Avenue and Manheim Street, for thirty years. He became a member of Ellis Post Six in 1879. He died on February 25, 1913, at age seventy-five. Interment was in Hood's Cemetery.

John B. Maxwell became proprietor of the General Wayne Inn after the war.

Inside the Hood Cemetery.

The entrance to the Hood Cemetery.

SERGEANT JOSEPH MAXWELL

Sergeant Joseph Maxwell enlisted when he was eighteen. He served throughout the war with the 150th Pennsylvania Volunteers, the famous Bucktails, and was twice wounded. He was mustered out as a second lieutenant.

After the war, Street Sergeant Maxwell became known all over Germantown because of his thirty-five-year service on the police force. He worked from the West Haines Street police station.

He died on July 21, 1909, at his home at 66 East Bringhurst Street. In attendance at the funeral were members of Mitchell Lodge 206, F&AM, Germantown Chapter 208, RAM, and Ellis Post Six, GAR; Germantown Republican Club; survivors of the Bucktails; and a detail from the Fourteenth District police station. He was interred in Ivy Hill Cemetery.

Joseph Maxwell became a police officer in Germantown after the war.

Musician Salvador Maxwell

When the war broke out, Salvador Maxwell enlisted as a musician in the band of the 114th Regiment Pennsylvania Volunteers.

After the war, he was appointed by Mayor Stokely to the position of patrolman in Germantown. He was a member of the old Germantown Band that was comprised of musicians from the different bands in the army; the organization disbanded in the late 1880s. He was also a member of Ellis Post Six, GAR, and several other organizations. He died in 1896.

Sergeant Peter McAnally

Sergeant Peter McAnally was born in Ireland in 1845 and immigrated to the United States at the age of eight. He fought with the Sixty-ninth Pennsylvania Volunteers in the war and was a sergeant in his company.

He was one of the most expert steel men in the country. For fifty years, he was connected with the Midvale Steel Company.

Mr. McAnally was a member of Ellis Post Six; the Sons of St. Patrick, the Knights of Columbus, and the British Iron and Steel Institute.

He died in December 1917. The funeral was held in the Catholic Church of St. Vincent de Paul, and interment was made in Cathedral Cemetery.

Private Joseph Meehan

Joseph Meehan, according to a December 1920 obituary listing in the *Independent-Gazette*, was born at Ryde, Isle of Wight, England, November 9, 1840. While there he received word from his brother Thomas that he had started a nursery at Germantown, Philadelphia, and that if Joseph wished to come out to him he would place him in charge of two or three greenhouses he had just erected. This being just the thing he wanted, in April 1859, he commenced his career as a nurseryman, a career which ended only after a connection of fifty-two years, when he retired altogether from nursery work. In that time the nursery had grown from the original three acres to about seventy acres, all within the city of Philadelphia.

While fairly well known as a nurseryman, it was as a writer on horticultural subjects that his fame chiefly rests. Some quarter of a century ago he saw what a financial help it would be to him in furthering his

Born in England, Joseph Meehan immigrated to the United States to join his brother's horticultural business in 1859.

ambition to secure himself and family in his older days, and he turned his attention to this line.

The Civil War attracted him in 1862, three years after landing in this country. He enlisted on August 13, in a three-year regiment, the 118th Pennsylvania Volunteers. The command of a thousand men was recruited in one month, starting at the end of July and ending the close of August. Such was the demand for reinforcements that one week later it was merged with the veterans of the 5th Corps and started with it on a long march ending with Antietam. It participated in that battle seventeen days after they left Philadelphia.

On September 20 the regiment suffered great loss at Shepherdstown, West Virginia, in following up Lee in his retreat from Antietam. Joseph Meehan was one of some 100 wounded, a ball entering his left shoulder. This was never extracted from behind his shoulder blade and caused his discharge in the winter of 1862–1863.

In June, 1863, when Lee again tried invading the North, Joseph Meehan again volunteered, this time in Landis's Battery of Light Artillery, an "emergency" organization. This command was in two engagements, one near Shiremantown, with Ewell's forces, which had been sent to capture Harrisburg, and another at Carlisle, Pa., when it refused to surrender the town to Stuart's Cavalry. In this action the battery had three wounded and one, Joseph Meehan, taken prisoner. Marched to Gettysburg he was there paroled on the field and on July 4, 1863, was returned to the Union forces together with several hundred other prisoners. He was then sent to Camp Parole, West Chester, Pa., where he remained until the battery returned to Philadelphia.

After the war he was a comrade of Ellis Post and was well known as one of the color sergeants of the Post and he had been known to declare that he had in that capacity carried the flag at the funeral of over a hundred colleagues who had gone before him to the cemetery.

Joseph Meehan died December 23, 1920, at his home, 121 Pleasant Street. Funeral services were conducted by the Rev. Stanley B. Wilcox, assistant rector of Gloria Dei (Old Swede's) Church. Grand Army services were also held by Ellis Post. The interment was in Ivy Hill Cemetery.

GENERAL GEORGE GORDON MEADE

General George Gordon Meade, a Philadelphian, and the victor in the battle of Gettysburg. He acquired some of his earliest military education in this neighborhood; in the 1830s, he was a student at the American Classical and Military Institute, which Colonel A.L. Roumford conducted at Mount Airy, on the site of the present Lutheran Theological Seminary. Military drill and discipline was a feature of the course of instruction in the school.

Colonel Roumford conducted his school from 1826 until 1836 in the mansion which William Allen—later chief justice of Pennsylvania—had built in about 1750. In 1807, a seminary had been opened in the Allen house by the Reverend Francis Xavier Brosius, a French Catholic priest, and in 1813, Roumford disposed of the school to Benjamin Constant, also a Frenchman, who called it a collegiate institute. A large number of pupils from the South and the West Indies attended at that time. Colonel Roumford, a native of France and a graduate of the West Point Military Academy, was an instructor in the school, and in 1826, he succeeded Constant as proprietor. He changed the name and made military training a feature.

There were seven to ten instructors, and the cadets wore a gray uniform, with white trousers in summer, and a cap with a bell crown seven inches high and adorned with a yellow cockade and an eagle. The uniform seemed to

General George Gordon Meade acquired some of his military education at the American Classical and Military Academy in Mount Airy (now the Lutheran Theological Seminary).

arouse the ire of the town boys and fights between them and the students were frequent. Military drills were held daily, and there were morning and evening parades. Troublesome pupils were confined in a guardhouse. Colonel Roumford, on retiring from the school in 1835, became military storekeeper in Philadelphia.

GENERAL JAMES ST. CLAIR MORTON

General James St. Clair Morton was born in Germantown on September 24, 1829, son of Dr. Samuel George and Rebecca Grellet (Pearsall) Morton. He attended the University of Pennsylvania from 1843 to 1846; graduated from the U.S. Military Academy, second in the class of 1851; and was assigned to the corps of engineers. He was assistant engineer in the construction of the defenses at Charleston, South Carolina, from 1851 to 1852, and in the building of Fort Delaware, Delaware, from 1852 to 1855. He was promoted on April 1, 1854, to second lieutenant in the corps of engineers; served as assistant professor of mathematics and military engineering at the U.S.

General James St. Clair Morton, a noted engineer, was killed at Petersburg in 1864.

Military Academy from 1855 to 1857; served as engineer in the preliminary work at Sandy Hook Fort, New Jersey, from 1857 to 1858; and built the Sandy Hook lighthouse. He was promoted on July 1, 1856, to first lieutenant; served as lighthouse engineer from 1858 to 1859; and had charge of work on the Washington Monument and was engineer of the Potomac water works from 1859 to 1860.

He was in command of the Chiriqui expedition to Central America in 1860 and was superintending engineer during the building of Fort Jefferson at Tortugas, Florida, from 1861 to 1862 and of repairs at Fort Mifflin, Pennsylvania, in 1862. He was promoted on August 6, 1861, as captain of the corps of engineers; served as chief engineer of the Army of the Ohio from May to October 1862; served as chief engineer of the Army of the Cumberland from October 1862 to November 1863; and commanded the Pioneer brigade attached to the fourteenth corps of the Army of the Cumberland. He was commissioned on November 29, 1862, as brigadier general of U.S. volunteers; and served in the Tennessee campaign, being engaged in the Battle of Stone's River from December 31, 1862, to January 3, 1863; was brevetted as a U.S. lieutenant colonel on January 2, 1863, for gallant and meritorious services in the battle of Stone's River; was engaged in fortifying Nashville and Murfreesboro, Tennessee, from January to June

1863; participated in the advance on Tullahoma from June to July 1863; and was promoted on July 8, 1863, to major.

He took part in the Battle of Chickamauga on September 19–20, 1863, where he was wounded; was brevetted on September 20, 1863, to colonel for gallant and meritorious services in that battle; and was engaged in fortifying Chattanooga from September to November 1863. He was mustered out of the volunteer service on November 7, 1863; served as superintending engineer of the defenses of Nashville, Murfreesboro, Clarksville and Fort Donelson from November 14, 1863, to January 30, 1864; was assistant to the chief engineer at Washington, D.C., from January to May 1864; and chief engineer of the Ninth Army Corps from May to June 1864. Morton was engaged in the Battle of North Anna on May 24, 1864; Battle of Tolopotomy on May 28–29, 1864; Battle of Bethesda Church on May 30, 1864; and the assault of Petersburg, Virginia, where he was killed on June 17, 1864, while leading the attack.

He was brevetted to brigadier general of the U.S. Army that same day for gallant and meritorious services at the assault on Petersburg. He is the author of "An Essay on Instruction in Engineering (1856)," an essay on "A New Plan for the Fortification of Certain Points of the Sea Coast of the United

The gatehouse to Laurel Hill Cemetery.

States (1858)," "Memoir on American Fortification (1859)," "Dangers and Defences of New York City (1858)" and "Life and Services of Major John Saunders of the Engineers (1860)."

He was buried with military honors at Laurel Hill Cemetery, Philadelphia.

COLONEL FREDERICK C. NEWHALL

Colonel Frederick C. Newhall was born on February 11, 1840, at the old Newhall homestead in Germantown as a member of the well-known Newhall family. He was educated at private schools in the city.

At the outbreak of the Civil War, Newhall enlisted in the Sixth Pennsylvania Cavalry, and rose to the rank of captain. After the Battle of Fredericksburg,

Colonel Frederic C. Newhall (right), seen with Major General Philip Sheridan (center) and Brigadier General James W. Forsyth.

he was made provost marshal of the Sixth Army Corps, and in 1865, he was appointed assistant adjutant general of the middle division with the rank of lieutenant colonel. This position he retained until the close of the war, and in the discharge of its incidental duties, he won the highest praise from his superior officers and the president himself.

After the war, Colonel Newhall returned to private life and became a member of the sugar-refining firm of McKean, Newhall & Borie; upon the dissolution of this firm, he represented the Franklin Sugar Refinery in New York and then went to London as the representative of the American Sugar Refining Company.

REVEREND EDWARD NEWS

An unusual circumstance was connected with the funeral of the Reverend Edward News at St. Vincent's Seminary on East Chelten Avenue; this Catholic priest was a member of the Grand Army of the Republic, and two members of Ellis Post Six took part in the funeral services as representatives of the Grand Army.

Father News fought as a private in the Seventy-third Pennsylvania Volunteers, Company G, at the time of the Civil War. This was, however, before he had become a priest. He was ordained in 1871 and was a member of the Congregation of the Mission, with the mother house at St. Vincent Seminary. At one time he was an assistant priest at the Church of St. Vincent de Paul on East Price Street, but for the fourteen years before his death, he was chaplain of St. Joseph's Hospital in Norfolk, Virginia. He died there on June 4, 1915, at age seventy-three.

When arrangements were made for the funeral, it transpired that Father News had joined a Grand Army post in Brooklyn before his ordination and had maintained his membership ever since, being proud to wear the bronze button of the Grand Army. The authorities of the seminary communicated with Theodore Schweriner, sergeant major of Ellis Post Six, and asked him to bring a delegation of the post to the funeral. Mr. Schweriner and the chaplain of the post, George W. Engle, were present at the solemn requiem Mass celebrated in the seminary chapel, and the flag of the post was draped over the casket of the dead priest.

None of the Grand Army ritual for the burial of the dead was used, but at the request of the Vincentian fathers, the two members of Ellis Post Six served as honorary pallbearers when the body of Father News was placed in the crypt under the main altar of the chapel. As the casket was closed,

Chaplain Engle placed a small United States flag inside the casket, as is the custom at the burial of soldiers.

After the funeral, Engle and Schweriner were shown through the seminary and were the guests of the seminary priests at dinner, at which many visiting priests were present. All the clergy took a special delight in greeting the two Grand Army veterans.

Father News was born on August 6, 1843, in Ireland.

PRIVATE RICHARD P. NICKUALS

Private Richard P. Nickuals enlisted in 1861 in the Seventy-first Pennsylvania Regiment, Company C. He received a gunshot wound in his right foot at the Battle of Ball Bluff and was discharged the following year. After the war, his occupation was brass clock maker.

GENERAL JOSHUA T. OWEN

General Joshua Owen was born on March 29, 1821, in Caermarthen, Wales, and immigrated to the United States with his parents in 1830. He graduated in 1845 from Jefferson College in Canonsburg, Pennsylvania, and was engaged in teaching and the practice of law, being admitted to

R.P. Nickuals, Seventy-first Pennsylvania Volunteers.

the bar in 1852. He established, with his brother Robert, the Chestnut Hill Academy for boys. He was a member of the state legislature from 1857 to 1859, was a private in the First City Troop of Philadelphia in 1861 and on May 8 of that year, he became colonel of the Twenty-fourth Pennsylvania Volunteers. After being mustered out after his three months' service, he organized on August 18, 1861, the Sixty-ninth Pennsylvania Regiment, of which he became colonel. With that regiment, he served in all the battles of the Army of the Potomac, from Fair Oaks to Cold Harbor, commanding a brigade part of the time and winning by gallant and meritorious conduct at Glendale a promotion to the rank of brigadier general of volunteers on November 29, 1862. His commission expired on March 4, 1863, but he was reappointed on March 30, and he served until mustered out July 18, 1864. General Owen then resumed the practice of his profession in Philadelphia and was recorder of deeds there from 1866 to 1871. Owen was also a member of MOLLUS (143).

General Owen died on November 7, 1887, in Chestnut Hill in Philadelphia.

General Joshua T. Owen, Twenty-fourth Pennsylvania Regiment.

GENERAL WILLIAM J. PALMER

General William J. Palmer, the founder of Colorado Springs, Colorado, was a former resident of Germantown. Before the Civil War, he lived at 513 High Street. He left to enter the army and attained distinction as commander of the Fifteenth Pennsylvania Cavalry, known as Anderson's Cavalry. A reunion of this regiment was held at General Palmer's home in August 1907. A millionaire, General Palmer paid all the expenses of the members' trip to the West. Howard A. Buzby, of 5153 Wakefield Street, and David C. King, of 111 East Upsal Street—Germantown survivors of the regiment—attended the reunion.

General Palmer died on March 13, 1909, and was buried in Evergreen Cemetery in El Paso County, Colorado.

COLONEL TATNALL PAULDING

Colonel Tatnall Paulding was born in July 1840 in Huntingdon, Long Island. He was attending West Point Military Academy when the Civil War began, and he immediately joined the Seventh New York Volunteers. In a few weeks' time, he was commissioned a lieutenant in the Sixth United

Colonel Tatnall Paulding became president of the Delaware Insurance Company.

States Cavalry, and he served with that command throughout the war, participating in various battles of the Army of the Potomac.

He was taken prisoner on the third day of the Battle of Gettysburg and spent nine months in Libby Prison. As soon as he was liberated, he rejoined his regiment and continued with it in active service until July 1866, when he came to live in Philadelphia; his father, Rear Admiral Hiram Paulding was then governor of the Naval Asylum in the city. In the meantime, Tatnall had been promoted through various ranks to that of lieutenant colonel by brevet. He was a grandson of the famous John Paulding, who was instrumental in the capture of Major John Andre during the Revolutionary War.

Paulding became president of the Delaware Insurance Company and was widely known in financial circles. He was a member of the Union League and MOLLUS (464).

Colonel Paulding died in March 1907 at his home at 152 West Penn Street. The funeral services were held in St. Luke's Episcopal Church, and the burial took place in St. Luke's Churchyard.

COLONEL RICHARD HENRY RUSH

Colonel Richard Henry Rush was a son of Richard Rush, of Philadelphia, and was born in England during the time his father was minister to the Court of St. James. He graduated from West Point in 1846. As lieutenant in the Second Artillery, he served with his regiment and as instructor in artillery at West Point until the commencement of the Mexican War, through which he served with great distinction.

At the time of the Civil War, Rush lived in the old Bensell house at Germantown Avenue at School House Lane, and in later years, he lived on Morris Street. On the outbreak of the Civil War in 1861, Rush, who had resigned from the regular army several years previously, urged Governor Curtin to immediately call out large bodies of troops. Later on, the Governor did so and placed Colonel Rush in command of the Sixth Pennsylvania Cavalry, a regiment largely raised by the colonel's efforts and officered by his personal friends. It was a regiment widely known throughout the war as "Rush's Lancers," of whom General McClellan said: "They are the eyes and ears of my army." The Lancers had a number of Germantown recruits, and its encampment was pitched there.

Colonel Rush was recommended several times for promotion to the rank of brigadier general, but owing to official and partisan jealousies, the recommendations were never acted upon. He served with his regiment during the arduous campaigns of the Peninsula and was finally ordered to Washington, where the chief command of the organization of the Veteran Reserve Corps was conferred upon him. Rush did much to bring the corps to a high degree of efficiency.

PRIVATE ADAM SANDERSON

Private Adam Sanderson was born on January 26, 1843, in North Andover, Massachusetts. He enlisted on April 29, 1861, in Company F, Fourteenth Regiment, Massachusetts Volunteer Infantry, ten days after Fort Sumter was fired upon. Later he served in the First Massachusetts Artillery and was wounded at Petersburg after a ball struck him in the pit of the stomach. He was taken from the battlefield in an almost lifeless condition. The wound troubled him for the rest of his life.

He was sent as a prisoner to Libby Prison, and then later to Andersonville, Mellon and Savannah, where he was paroled, subsequently going to Annapolis. He was honorably discharged from the army at Boston in February 1865.

Sergeant Sanderson came to Germantown in 1865, where he lived from then on. He was appointed in July 1873 as a patrolman and was made sergeant March 8, 1884. His record as a police official is second only to his record as a soldier, and he was widely known throughout the Twenty-second Ward. From 1917 to 1920, he was in command of the Chestnut Hill substation.

Sanderson moved from his home at 203 East Phil-Ellena Street to the Soldiers' Home in Erie, Pennsylvania, after the death of his wife. He was eighty years old at his death in 1922. At that time, he was post commander of Ellis Post Six, GAR.

PRIVATE THEODORE G.H. SCHWERINER

Almost every Germantowner knew Theodore Schweriner, who conducted the *Independent-Gazette*'s Grand Army Chat and fought for Uncle Sam in the Civil War. But it might have surprised even some of his intimate friends to learn that he also had some thrilling experiences with Indians in the wild and West.

He arrived in this country from Germany, then a boy of fifteen. For a few years, he remained with an uncle in Chicago; he then worked in a furrier's establishment in Peoria, Illinois, and enlisted at that place in the army.

Schweriner served in the Eighth Missouri Regiment, though prior to enlistment he had never been in the state of Missouri and indeed had not known that there was such a state. Illinois's quota of soldiers had already been supplied, so the captain took the company down to St. Louis, Missouri, and enlisted them in the Eighth Missouri. Enlistment was not brisk in Missouri, and the Eighth Missouri Regiment had only three companies of Missourians, the remainder and most of the officers—including the colonel—coming from Illinois. During the three years that he was in the service, Schweriner accompanied his regiment through Missouri, Kentucky, Tennessee, Mississippi, Louisiana, Alabama, Georgia and Arkansas. He was twice wounded, once in the left arm, at the siege of Vicksburg, and again at Arkansas Post, Arkansas, when a bullet grazed his head.

After the war, he was employed in a clothing store in Hannibal, Missouri, Mark Twain's old home. While there, he sang in the choir of the Congregational Church and also "called off" at village dances, being the most popular manager of dances in the region.

After a few years, he, like many other young men of that time, yielded to the lure of the gold regions of the West. With several hundred dollars that he had saved, he bought a wagon and a miner's outfit, and with a party of men having similar objects in view, he set out along the Santa Fe Trail—the great highway to the Southwest.

He said of his adventures:

> We didn't get much gold, and when our supplies ran out we went to work in a saw-mill out in the wilds of New Mexico. The Indians were causing much trouble throughout the region at that time, and we had a military guard at the mill, while wagon trains traveling through the country had to have cavalry escorts if they wanted to reach their destination in safety.
>
> One day a big wagon train of lumber left our mill, but no soldiers were at hand to accompany it. The next morning several of the mules that had been attached to the wagons came back to the mill. That told us that trouble was brewing.
>
> All hands were put under arms and we waited in the greatest anxiety, expecting any moment that we would be attacked. Some hours later, along a trail on the side of a mountain five or six miles away, we saw a

long procession of the Indians passing in single file, as is their custom. In the middle of the procession they had the mules from the wagon train that had not escaped. They made no attempt to disturb us, and when the soldiers came to our aid and we were able to send out a party along the trail we found the wagon train in ashes, the [Indians] having set it on fire. Nothing was ever heard as to the fate of the men accompanying the wagons.

Schweriner (known as T.S.) came to Germantown in 1882 and was a shoe merchant for many years at 5725 Germantown Avenue. As most of the survivors of his regiment lived in the West, he rarely met them. At the last reunion the regiment held, in 1900 in Chicago, he was elected president, and as no more reunions were expected, he was considered the permanent president of the regiment's survivors.

Schweriner, of 54 West Chelten Avenue, died on December 1, 1915, in his seventy-third year in the Jewish Hospital (now the Einstein Medical Center). Relatives and friends, also Ellis Post Six, GAR, Masonic Veterans of Pennsylvania, and Court Germantown 53, F. of A., were invited to attend the funeral from his brother's residence, 5805 McMahon Avenue. Interment was at Adath Jeshurun Cemetery.

CAPTAIN JOHN H. SHINGLE

Captain John H. Shingle was born in Germantown and died in August 1907 at Leavenworth, Kansas. He was a member of the Ninety-fifth Pennsylvania Regiment and was a Medal of Honor recipient.

SECOND LIEUTENANT HOWARD SHIPLEY

Second Lieutenant Howard Shipley was born in Germantown in 1844 at Chelten and Wayne Avenues. He enlisted in the Ninety-first Regiment at the age of sixteen. Then he joined the Twentieth Pennsylvania Volunteers and took part in many engagements; he was severely wounded in one of those battles. In later years, he was a manufacturer of pocket cutlery. He lived at 222 West Penn Street and was interred at Calvary Church.

Lieutenant Howard W. Shipley
was born in a house at Chelten
and Wayne Avenues.

First Lieutenant George W. Shriver

First Lieutenant George W. Shriver enlisted on August 15, 1862, as a private in Company B, 119th Pennsylvania Volunteers, and was promoted as follows: corporal, January 12, 1863; first sergeant, September 1, 1863; and first lieutenant, July 25, 1864. He was discharged on June 19, 1865.

He had a noteworthy record as a soldier in the Civil War, having fought in nineteen battles. He was twice wounded, first on April 2, 1862, at Petersburg, Virginia, and again at Fort Stedman, just three years later to the day. Besides these two, he participated in the following battles: Antietam, White Oak Church, Marye's Heights, Gettysburg, Hagerstown, Rappahannock Station, Mine Run, Wilderness, Spotsylvania, Cold Harbor and Winchester.

He lived his entire life on East Haines Street. Historian Namaan K. Ployd, who served in the same regiment, said:

Haines Street gave over one hundred of its boys and men when President Lincoln called for troops to defend the flag of the nation. The Shriver families were conspicuous. The John Shriver family gave three sons for the war, Reuben, William, and George. Reuben and William gave their lives early, while George, carrying a painful wound, lived till he was 71.

These heroic boys were great-grandchildren of Captain John Miller, of lower Germantown, who fell fighting for freedom under the illustrious General Washington. Well do I remember George W. Shriver, George C. Humes, E.T. Nice and the Ployd brothers, of old Haines street, hurrying to the camp of the 119th Pennsylvania Volunteers at Feltonville to be enrolled in Company B, all under the command of the great soldier, Colonel P.C. Ellmaker.

Soon this big regiment was hurried to the Capital. And then commenced the march to Fredericksburg, and from that disastrous battle to Appomattox. It was one of blood and carnage and many went down to death, while thousands received wounds and disease to carry to the grave.

Of the little band of Haines Street boys who battled in Company B, Humes, risen from a private to the command of the company, fell at Cold Harbor; Nice, promoted to a sergeancy, fell at Spotsylvania; George W. Shriver, risen to a lieutenancy, and his cousin, William Ployd, to the position of orderly sergeant, both fell dangerously wounded at Petersburg, Va., and both were carried from that bloody field to carry their wounds to the grave, but in reunited country.

Shriver died on March 8, 1913, at his home at 42 East Haines Street. Interment was made at Ivy Hill Cemetery. Ellis Post Six, Grand Army of the Republic, of which he was a member, conducted services at the grave.

MAJOR POWELL STACKHOUSE

Major Powell Stackhouse was born on July 16, 1840, in Philadelphia, the son of Joseph D. and Sarah P. Stackhouse, both Friends (Quakers). In April 1861, he enlisted in the Johnstown, Pennsylvania, Zouave Cadets, served through the war with the 198th Pennsylvania Regiment and was a major of a battalion.

He was later the president of the Mahoning Ore and Steel Company, the Penn Iron Mining Company, the president of the Cambria Steel Company

The Pennsylvania State Historic Marker for Laurel Hill Cemetery.

and the first vice president of the American Iron and Steel Institute. Stackhouse was also a member of MOLLUS (Registry 202).

Major Stackhouse died on February 4, 1927, in St. Petersburg, Florida. His house in Germantown was at 240 West Tulpehocken Street. He was buried in West Laurel Hill Cemetery.

First Lieutenant William Tourison

First Lieutenant William Tourison was born in 1839 and was killed on July 3, 1863, at Gettysburg. He served in the Twenty-eighth Pennsylvania Regiment, Company E. He was buried in St. Michael's Lutheran Churchyard.

William H. Tourison was killed at Gettysburg.

CAPTAIN ANTON VON UTASSY

Von Utassy was born in 1833 in Budapest, Hungary. On account of the Hungarian Revolution of 1848—in which his family, who belonged to the nobility, took an active part—he was forced to leave Hungary and went to Paris to finish his education.

At the outbreak of the Civil War, he came to this country and received a commission as captain, serving under General Fremont and Company F, Thirty-ninth New York Infantry, the Garibaldi Guard.

After the war was over, he entered the lumber business in Philadelphia and lived after that in Germantown. He was a member of the Union League, Art Club, Germantown Cricket Club and other organizations.

He died on February, 11, 1911, at his home at 6015 Greene Street and was interred in Ivy Hill Cemetery.

GENERAL LOUIS WAGNER

General Louis Wagner was born on August 4, 1838, in Giessen, in what is now Germany, and he came to the United States with his parents after the revolutions of 1848, which occurred throughout Europe, especially in the various German political divisions. At the outbreak of the Civil War, he enlisted in the Eighty-eighth Pennsylvania Volunteers as a first lieutenant. He was promoted to the rank of captain; in 1862, to lieutenant colonel; then colonel; and, at the end of the war, he was made a brigadier general.

He was wounded and taken prisoner on August 30, 1862, at the second Battle of Bull Run and was paroled on the field. His wound resulted in permanent disability, and he was sent home before the Battle at Chancellorsville.

He asked to be given the command of Camp William Penn at Chelten Hills, now La Mott. He asked the Union League to support the raising of five black regiments. More than fourteen thousand troops were trained at Camp William Penn.

After the war, he became interested in politics, first entering the city council. At the expiration of his third term, he was appointed a member of the board of education and served three years. He then ran again for city council and was elected; he was elected president of the council three times. Mayor Edward H. Fitler appointed him to organize the department

General Louis Wagner (center front) commanded Camp William Penn, where African American troops were trained. He is seen here with his staff.

General Louis Wagner.

of public works. He also served on the board of city trusts, starting in 1875, and was president of the board when he died.

He was greatly interested in Girard College, and his scrapbooks (in the collection of the Germantown Historical Society) have many references to the college.

The first suggestion for the erection of the soldiers' monument in Market Square is attributed to General Wagner. After the death of Benjamin Allen, the first chairman of the monument committee, General Wagner became chairman of the committee, and he gave important aid in raising the money to pay for the memorial. At the time of the dedication of the monument on July 4, 1883, he had a prominent part in the exercises. After the erection of the monument, General Wagner was chairman of the citizens' committee that cared for it and attended to inscribing the names of dead soldiers on the tablets.

The general was very active in the Market Square Presbyterian Church and organized the church's Bible class. Never, if he could avoid it, did he miss attending a Sunday morning service or a Wednesday evening prayer meeting. The night before his death, he was present at the services in his church. He was also a teacher in the Market Square Church's Sunday school.

General Wagner died on January 15, 1914. The honorary pallbearers at his funeral were chosen as representatives of the many bodies with which General Wagner had been connected, in addition to E.T. Stotesbury, who was one of his oldest personal friends. The list includes former Governor Edwin S. Stuart, Mayor Blankenburg, Controller Walton, George W. Kendrick Jr., Thomas J. Budd, William H. Scott, M.M. Eavenson, General Robert B. Beath, General Thomas J. Stewart, William H, Dempster, Dr. Chessman A. Herrick, William T. Tilden, Daniel W. Bussinger, Gavin Neilson, C.J. Hexamer, William J. Wells and the presiding officer of each of the Masonic bodies of which General Wagner was a member. Interment was at Ivy Hill Cemetery, with Masonic and GAR ceremonies.

General Louis Wagner's funeral on January 18, 1914.

THE WISTER FAMILY

Colonel Francis Wister

Francis Wister, fifth son of William and Sarah Logan (Fisher) Wister, was born on June 2, 1841, at the old family mansion—Belfield—in Germantown. Francis Wister was educated at Germantown Academy and the University of Pennsylvania, graduating at the latter institution class of 1860. He responded to the first call for volunteers to put down the rebellion and was commissioned captain on August 5, 1861, in the 12th Regiment, U.S. Infantry. He was promoted on April 21, 1865, to colonel of the 215th Regiment, Pennsylvania Volunteers; was mustered out of the volunteer service on August 28, 1865; and resigned from regular army service on April 5, 1866. While serving with the 12th U.S. Infantry, he was brevetted on May 3, 1863, as major for gallant and meritorious service at the Battle of Chancellorsville, and on July 2, 1863, he was brevetted lieutenant colonel for gallant and meritorious service at the Battle of Gettysburg. Francis was a member of MOLLUS (2587).

He died on November 25, 1905.

Jones Wister

Jones Wister was a member of the Pennsylvania militia in 1863.

Colonel Langhorne Wister

Colonel Langhorne Wister, was in the 150th Pennsylvania Regiment, Bucktails, and a member of MOLLUS (2344).

Rodman Wister

Rodman Wister was the youngest son of William and Sarah Logan Fisher Wister, and was born on August 10, 1844, at Belfield. When the Civil War began, he enlisted as a drummer boy in Captain Biddle's company, the Home Guards, of Germantown. Transferred to the Eighth Regiment, Pennsylvania Militia, he served through the Antietam campaign. An attack of typhoid fever in 1863 resulted in his honorable discharge.

He was president of the Duncannon Iron Company and a member and officer in many charitable organizations. A member of one of the oldest

Philadelphia families, prominent in club and social life, Wister was one of the men who introduced the game of cricket to this country.

He died on August 4, 1913, at age seventy-three in the Media Hospital in Media, Pennsylvania.

Colonel William Rotch Wister

Colonel William Rotch Wister was born on December 7, 1827, to William and Sarah Wister on the Wister estate. He studied law at the University of Pennsylvania. He was one of the founders of the Germantown Cricket Club.

At the outbreak of the Civil War, Wister followed in the footsteps of his ancestors and went to the front as lieutenant colonel of the Twentieth Pennsylvania Cavalry, where he won distinction as a formidable foe to the Confederacy. William was a member of MOLLUS (11945).

CONFEDERATES

Only five Confederate soldiers from Germantown are known: George Lehman Ashmead, Texas; Andrew R. Bebler, Second Virginia Cavalry; Jacob Hortter Bechtel; Thomas Comfort, Louisiana Tigers Regiment; and Benjamin Franklin White, Physician Confederate Army.

CHAPTER 4

Two Letters from the Front

JOHN MIDDLETON TO HIS WIFE, MARY

John B. Middleton joined the Union army on August 23, 1861, in Philadelphia, training along with his unit, the 95th Regiment of the Pennsylvania Volunteers, the Gosline Zouaves. He wrote the following letter from the battlefield in June 1862 in the fairly tranquil days before battle. It is one of nearly seventy letters he wrote to his wife, Mary, during his brief service. After the war, he was a Germantown mail carrier for many years.

Afternoon June 15, 1862

My Dearest Wife and Boy,

I am sorry indeed to hear that the poor little fellow [is ill] *but it is warm weather & not so much danger of catching cold & I trust you will take good care of him as you have done before. Now the order is given to stack our tents ready to move about one quarter of a mile on to a niew ground for our health as we have bin here on this ground for three weeks twelve o'clock today. The ground where we are going to camp is a high & dry place plenty of good water & a woods along sid of us. I am well as usual so are all of the Germantown Boyes except Ellwood Lefferts but he is getting better. John Ma…is well & is one of the cooks at present. Mr. Boyed is well and wishes to be remembered to you & his sisters & the little nieces you spoke of.*

Picket Post Monday morning tenn o'clock

June 16th 1862 in Hanover Co. Va.

At the Front by George Cochran Lambdin, a 1686 oil on canvas. One of the Germantown artist's few Civil War paintings. The figure may be his brother Harry. *Courtesy of the Detroit Institute of Arts, Founders Society Purchase, Director's Discretionary Fund.*

This fine Monday morning finds me out with Company E. on Picket but no duty to perform as the whole reg[iment]t is out on Picket. If only half the regt. goes out then I stay in camp but this is the third time the regt. & I have bin out and Company E is always bin on the same Post & in the edge of a nice shady woods but more than half a mile from our Camp ground & if we had some pies and cakes and Lemonade it would seem more like a picknick than any picket duty. Our rashions are cooked by our cooks & carried out to us by them. We have bin getting two rashions of whiskey every day for the last month (I have a bottle & have gathered a lot of Snake root & put it into the bottle then I put my whiskey with it & drink it as a blood purifier & it does me good in two wayes). You see I have a lot of the root in my knapsack to bring home if I am lucky enough to get home to you & Joey againe & I expect to do so at Present.

I had almost forgot to say that I receveid a letter on last Wednesday the eleventh (no. 62) and on my bearth day I was out with the Co. on picket that day & I asked the good man to make me a better man for the next year

Two Letters from the Front

Quartermaster's Department mail wagon during the Civil War in 1865. The nearly seventy letters John Middleton and his wife exchanged during his brief service would have been delivered this way. *Courtesy Print and Picture Collection, Free Library of Philadelphia.*

to come & before another bearth day shall come around I hope to be at home with you and Joey to live in peace & happiness the balance of our lives. I am satisfied now that I did know that the happiness of a home & a wife & a sweet little boy to love was but my dearest [wish]. *I can appreciate it now in my minde & always shall as long as I live. I receveid two stamps in letter no. 62 I am very much obliged to you for them. I receveid a letter from George and Jane* [McCullough, his brother-in-law and sister] *last week with a stamp & I answered it right off & I sent my love to you in it.*

The Co. don't like the niew Capt. He has to go to the Preists of the 3rd New York regt. almost every morning. He is a mean little [illegible] *as ever lived & has not a friend in the Co. not even the Lieutenants don't like him. He has given them both orders not* [to] *speak to or talk to the privets in the Co. and when in command, but he is not obeyed by either of them in that respect. They say they will be social & agreable with the Co. if they get discharged for it, so Robberts told me the other day. Some of the boyes have saide what they would do in case the Capt. ever had to take them skirmishing through the woods in time of a battle.*

It is all right in sending for Dr. Malin for Joey for it is the safest plan to know in time. I am glad to heare of Michel Carles coming back in one respect but sorry in another for if I was at home now I should not care to come back againe. I am glad for the tobacco & the handker[chief] & the zinger but I am sorry to heare that you are so neare out of money for I am in the same fix. The Sutler [a person who follows an army and sells provisions to the soldiers] *is in camp now & some day we will be paid off soon & I hope it is true. Then I will send you some of it for I know you kneed it bad—for there is almost foure months wages due us or will be the first of July & another thing is I am afraid we will not spend the fourth of July together this yeare but never minde any other day of the yeare will be just as good to us as the fourth would be. If I only live to see you both once more I will feel very thankful all the days of my life to come.*

Those cotton socks will be just the things I need this hot weather. I will pay Michel for his trouble when he gets into camp. I am very much obliged to you for the Camden niews. We heard of Capt. Acuff being wounded before the papers published as some of the troops that wher in the battle wher in our camp in two days of the battle & told us of it. When you write to Mrs. Myer give them my love & all the rest of the fokes & let me know where aunt Emily is the next time you write. When you see or write to hir give hir my love. Now I will stop writing till tomorrow when we go into camp so I can maile it. So good by my most loved ones at home. May the good mans care & protection be with you & poor little Joey do take care of him. I often look at your faces in the amber tips [ambrotype photos] *& wish my self with you both at home. May god bless you both is my prayer.*

Middleton wrote this letter in the quiet days before the Battle of Gaines's Mill, Virginia (also known as the First Battle of Cold Harbor). He was wounded in the battle; a rifle ball passed through his right arm. The Ninety-fifth Pennsylvania Volunteers bore heavy casualties, with every second officer and man killed or wounded. Civilians took care of the wounded near the battlefield, but the soldiers had a better chance of survival at one of the hospitals. Middleton was fortunate to be sent to Cuyler Hospital in Germantown. There were no antibiotics or knowledge about germs, but some nurses and hospitals made a significant effort to keep the patients and buildings clean. Some nurses had training but they were all volunteers. Commissary planning for the number of wounded was poor, so Middleton was lucky to reach Philadelphia where there were doctors and nurses to treat him. He unfortunately contracted chronic pleurisy while doing guard duty at Cuyler after recovering from his wounds.

Captain Francis Acuff (or Achuff) was wounded and discharged in April 1863. He died in 1865.

A Battlefield Letter from George Shriver

Among the hundred or more men who enlisted in the Union army from East Haines Street were George W. Shriver and George Humes. They, together with Naaman K. Ployd and William Ployd, joined Company B, 119th Regiment, Pennsylvania Volunteers. In the Battle of Cold Harbor on June 3, 1864, Humes was killed, and Shriver wrote a letter to his comrade's mother in Germantown, conveying the sad news:

> *In the field near Cold Harbor Tavern, June 4, 1864:*
>> *Dear Cousin:*
>>> *I take my pencil to inform you of the death of George. He was killed on the 3d with a solid shot, about half-past 10 o'clock in the morning. He was killed instantly. He was taken to the rear and buried as well as it could be done. The orderly sergeant, with four men, buried him. I would have gone with them, but I could not get off, for we had just advanced to the position where we are now lying. It is about sixty yards from the enemy's works. His things that he had in his pockets are all safe, and as soon as I can get a chance I will send them to you. If there is anything that you want to know concerning him, please let me know and I will do all I can for you. At the time he was killed he was acting adjutant of the regiment. There is one thing that belonged to him I would like to have, and that is his haversack. I don't want you to give it to me for nothing for I will buy it from you. I will have to close by sending my love to all.*
>> *Yours truly,*
>> *George W. Shriver*

This letter, which George W. Shriver wrote on the battlefield to tell a Germantown mother of the death of her son in battle, came back into his hands in 1929. It was found among the effects of Mrs. Sarah Humes, after her death at her home on Haines Street. The executors of her estate gave it to Mr. Shriver.

The solid shot that killed George Humes was an enormous six-pound ball. It struck a limb of a tree over his head, which swerved its course downward, so that it penetrated Humes's body at the shoulder and made its way through his chest. When he was buried, the ball was placed in the grave with him. At the close of the war, his body was disinterred and, together with the fatal ball, was brought to Germantown. The body was buried in the cemetery of the Haines Street Methodist Church (later the Harmer Public

George Humes was buried in Ivy Hill Cemetery.

School). The body was removed to Ivy Hill Cemetery at a later date. The ball was afterward placed in the museum of Ellis Post Six, Grand Army of the Republic, in Town Hall.

The information from this passage is from a newspaper article on September 29, 1929.

CHAPTER 5

The Home Front

Hospitals

There were two hospitals in Germantown during the Civil War, the Mower Hospital in Chestnut Hill and the Cuyler Hospital in Germantown. The hospitals were staffed by dedicated doctors and nurses and supported by local residents' efforts.

Mower General Hospital

The Mower Hospital was located where the Wyndmoor Train Station (SEPTA Chestnut Hill East) is now, on Willow Grove Avenue near Stenton Avenue. It was one of the largest hospitals in the country with a capacity of 3,600 patients, according to a 1913 Naaman K. Ployd article. Its fifty wards were arranged as corridors that radiated as spokes on a wheel from a central corridor, with about fifty to one hundred beds per ward. It was also considered to be one of the most efficient hospitals. It opened on January 3, 1863, and continued until May 31, 1865. Of the approximately 20,000 admissions, 9,799 returned to duty; 1,363 were discharged; 3,718 were transferred; 1,508 deserted; 257 died; and 874 were transferred to the Veteran Reserve Corps.

Andrew Hopkins, MD, was the first surgeon general of the Mower Hospital. He died of typhoid fever at the end of the war. Mower Hospital was named for Thomas Mower, an early army surgeon. It was originally known as Chestnut Hill Hospital. Patients were brought directly from the battlefield by trains with special cars.

Mower Hospital (Chestnut Hill) parade ground.

Mower Hospital from the observatory.

The stone water tower owned by the Chestnut Hill Water Company on Ardleigh Street, which still exists, was used to supply fresh water to the hospital. The hospital was very clean, and it was washed frequently, although the concept of infection was not well understood.

The hospital was designed by architect John McArthur Jr., who also designed Philadelphia City Hall, and it was built on a tract of twenty-seven acres, extending from the railroad to Stenton Avenue and from Abington to Springfield Avenues.

The hospital buildings were constructed of wood, lined with dressed boards inside, while the outer surface was of lath and plaster. There were fifty pavilions, extending from a "corridor" 2,400 feet long and enclosing a space of seven acres. In the center of this space were the administration building, the chapel, post office, barber shop, band's quarters, band stand, dining hall for attendants, boiler house, engine room, conservatory, kitchens, carpenter shop, operating room, dead house, guard house, a sutler's (supplier) shop and various similar departments.

Barracks were built at the northeast corner of the tract for convalescents not under medical treatment and for the officers of the Veteran Reserve Corps, while at the northwest were the general dining room and barracks for the Veteran Reserve Corps guard.

For protection against fire, a fire-alarm telegraph system was established, and there were 3 hose carriages carrying 4,000 feet of hose, along with 1,200 fire buckets, 200 fire axes, 24 ladders and a stationary fire pump that were available.

A.B. Kerper, of Chestnut Hill, was commissary of the hospital. His records show that 100 dozen eggs and a four-wheeled car load of ice were consumed daily, while the milk bill averaged three hundred dollars a month. At a Thanksgiving feast at the hospital in 1864, the table extended the entire length of the "corridor"—about a half-mile—and the 3,500 soldiers present consumed the following: 2 tons of turkeys, 30,000 oysters, 25 bushels of potatoes, 3 barrels of beans, 4 barrels of crackers, 5 barrels of cranberries, a 1/2-ton of bread, 500 gallons of coffee, 1,200 quarts of milk, 225 pounds of butter and 800 quarts of ice cream.

"Reminiscences of Mower Hospital after the Battle of Gettysburg"

By T.L. Gregory

It was a week before the doctors at the hospital decided to operate to remove the bullets from my wound. Three doctors came up to the ward to my bed.

After asking my name, one of the doctors said they had come to take the bullet out of my arm. One of the doctors began shaking a bottle of ether, with a sponge over the bottle when I made the remark that I didn't want to take any ether or anything else to have the bullet taken out. The doctor who performed the operation thought that I had better take the ether, but I said, "No, I didn't take ether to get the lead in my arm and…me if I would take any of it to get the lead out."

The doctor felt around my arm and finally said there was no lead in it, but I insisted there was and he finally cut deep into the bone, putting his finger in the cut to draw the bullet out, but could not find it. Then after more argument with him he cut crosswise and inserted an instrument like a buttonhook, striking the lead.

Until that he had not hurt me, but when the lead was removed it hurt so badly that I hollered—anyone could have heard me a half-mile away. "Hold on, now," the doctor said "it will soon be over." The he stitched up the cuts and bandaged my arm, and said, "Now you can get up."

When he first struck the lead he threw it across the room, and the first thing that I did was to go over and pick it up. Doc said, "What are you going to do with it?" I told him I wanted it as a pocket piece. He asked me to show it to him and then said, "You'll do, all right!"

I suppose I will have to stay here until the surgeon in charge tells me I can leave. It's an all right place, but I prefer being with the boys and having a look at the beauties of nature. Of course, I know something of the use you are put to while in the hospital. In 1861 I was in one for three months for a wound that I received near Munison Hill in Virginia, so you can see I am not a novice in the hospital business. You are treated all right as long as you obey orders. If you don't then you are treated in proportion to your neglect of orders.

There were lots of visitors every day, so the time passed pleasantly. In fact it was so pleasant that three months had gone before I was fit for the front once more. While in the hospital I used to receive letters from the boys in the company, so that I had news from the front at least once a week, and that was something to be proud of.

When a new lot of wounded comes in from the front, you can see all sorts of wounds. I had been here about six weeks, and there were a lot of wounded came here from Gettysburg. There were fifty-one in the lot that only had fifty-one legs. Should have 102 to make up the usual complement of legs but they were short a few, but as gay a crowd of soldiers as ever I had seen. They used to get out on the parade grounds at the hospital. It would do anyone good to see the antics they used to cut up. The legs had all been amputated while in the hospital at Gettysburg, and as soon as the men were able to move they were sent to Philadelphia and landed at Chestnut Hill Hospital to get better, so that they could be discharged as unfit for duty. They didn't want any one-legged soldiers at the front. It was all you wanted to do to get around in your place with two legs.

As soon as my doctor told me I would be ready in a few days for the front, I asked him to send me that day. I thought that I was ready, but he said no, that I would have to go under an examination, and if I was ready to go, they would not keep me, for they wanted sound men at the front.

At last I left the hospital to rejoin the regiment. Once more there was quite a crowd of us left the hospital this morning for the front—some to be badly frightened, some to lay down their lives for their love of country. We were formed into a company and taken to the provost marshal's office at Fifth and Buttonwood Streets. We were arranged according to the provost's orders and then were sent to the Broad and Prime streets depot. From there we went to Washington, where we were fed and then sent under guard to Camp Convalescent to await our turn to be sent to our different regiments.

This letter appeared in a 1911 edition of the *Frankford Dispatch* and was republished in the *Germantown Independent Gazette* in 1913.

General and Surgeon Charles H. Greenleaf

Charles Greenleaf was born in 1838 in Carlisle, Pennsylvania. He was educated in Boston and Cincinnati, receiving his medical degree from the Ohio State Medical College in 1860. He was the first surgeon commissioned from Ohio in the Civil War. After serving in various commands, he was appointed to Philadelphia where, in 1862, he built the Mower General Hospital in Chestnut Hill, of which he served for a time as executive officer. After the Battle of Antietam, he became medical director of the army.

Later, General Greenleaf was the chief medical officer during the Pittsburgh riots of 1876; served on Indian campaigns and as executive officer in the surgeon general's office in Washington; and organized the Hospital Corps of the United States Army.

In 1902, he was brevetted brigadier general. General Greenleaf was the author of the present system for personal identification of soldiers in the United States Army and wrote many articles of note on this and kindred topics. He was also a member of MOLLUS (3073).

He died in September 1911, in San Jose, California.

CUYLER ARMY HOSPITAL

In the year 1862, the city of Philadelphia offered the Town Hall of Germantown to the United States government for hospital purposes. Under the influence of a number of patriotic ladies, Dr. James Darrach went to Washington and obtained from the surgeon general an order to the medical director of this district. According to the Reverend S. Hotchkin's *Ancient and Modern Germantown, Mount Airy and Chestnut Hill*, 1889, in July of the same year, the hospital was organized, with Dr. Darrach as surgeon in charge, and Drs. J.M. Leedom, W.R. Dunton, T.F. Betton, R.N. Downs, C.R. Prall, W. Darrach Jr., Horace Y. Evans, John Ashhurst Jr. and P.D. Keyser as assistant surgeons. The capacity of the original building being too limited, additions were made that enabled the hospital to accommodate 630 beds. About this time, it received the name of Cuyler Hospital in honor of John M. Cuyler, M.D., medical director, U.S. Army.

The ladies of Germantown continued to take an active interest in the hospital, and through their efforts a contribution room was established where delicacies were supplied daily to the sick and wounded soldiers. About a year after the organization of the hospital, Dr. Darrach resigned, and he was followed by Dr. Josiah Curtis, U.S. Volunteers, and Dr. H.S.

Cuyler Hospital was behind the Town Hall in Germantown.

Shell, U.S. Army. The hospital continued to receive patients until the end of the war and served a good purpose in receiving convalescent patients from the field hospitals, making room for those who needed prompt attention near the battlefield. The hospital was closed at the end of the war, and the remaining patients were transferred to the Mower Hospital in Chestnut Hill.

Following the Battle of Gettysburg, hundreds of wounded soldiers were brought to Philadelphia and placed in the various military hospitals of the city. Besides using the town hall, a number of frame buildings were put up in the rear, where the police station and the Germantown Boys Combined School later stood. In this way, space was provided for 630 beds.

Some amusing experiences at the town hall hospital were recalled by Mellville H. Freas, a survivor of the Bucktails, who lived on East Haines Street, and who was in the hospital in 1864, following his release from Confederate prisons.

Naaman K. Ployd wrote in the *Germantown Independent Gazette* in 1913 that, at Christmas time in 1864, the patients at the hospital had a great feast. About one hundred mince pies were left over, and Dr. Schell, who was in charge of the hospital, placed these in his storeroom. One day, George Benson, master of one of the wards, called Freas into his room and produced a mince pie that he had concealed in his bedding. The two disposed of the pie. "Where did you get it?" asked Freas. Benson pointed to a transom over the door entering the doctor's store room and whispered: "We smelled the pies and put little Jimmie through the transom and he passed them out."

Soon Dr. Schell's butler reported to him that the pies were disappearing rapidly, and the doctor summoned his various subordinates and questioned them closely, but none knew anything about the pies. However, the supply of pies continued to diminish. The pies were all on tin plates. One member of the invalid corps who lived on Centre Street (now Rittenhouse Street) and went home every evening used to carry away a pile of the plates with him, concealed under his coat and "sail" them into the gardens of the Eagle and Keyser homesteads. The butler came in and reported: "Doctor, I've found out what become of them pies—your horses are eating them." "How do you make that out?" demanded the doctor.

"Well," he replied, "when I went into the stable this morning, I found a half dozen empty pie plates with the horses."

Dr. Thomas F. Betton

For several decades in the middle of the nineteenth century, Dr. Thomas F. Betton was Germantown's foremost surgeon, and he was also active in public affairs generally. Dr. Betton was a son of Dr. Samuel Betton, who lived in the "White Cottage" that stood on Manheim Street near Greene Street. The son, who was born in 1809, built a house adjoining, where he lived the greater part of his life.

According to a *Germantown Independent Gazette* article, as early as 1832, Dr. Betton attained distinction, with the guardians of the poor of Philadelphia awarding him a certificate that year for his courage and professional skill displayed in caring for destitute victims of a cholera epidemic in the city. He was then a physician at one of the emergency hospitals. Dr. Betton was a leading spirit in the Independent Order of Odd Fellows, being a member of Philomathean Lodge of Germantown. He was chairman of the lodge's committee that built the hall still standing on Wister Street, and he delivered the address at the laying of the cornerstone of the hall in 1846. He served for many years in the sectional school board. At the time of the Civil War, Dr. Betton was a military surgeon, and his professional skill was highly regarded. He died in 1875. By his will, his library was bequeathed to the Philadelphia College of Physicians.

Nurse Catharine Keyser

Catharine Keyser was the daughter of Reuben Keyser, who was a business man in Germantown as early as 1820. Miss Keyser was born in 1845 and was educated in the Old Concord School House at Germantown Avenue and Washington Lane. During the Civil War, when town hall was converted into Cuyler Hospital, Miss Keyser acted as a nurse to the wounded soldiers of the Union army who were brought there. Miss Keyser was a descendant of Dirck Keyser, who came here in 1688. She was a life member of the First Presbyterian Church. She died on April 12, 1910, at age sixty-five.

Nurse Sarah Grier Beck

Mrs. Sarah G.R. Beck, daughter of Robert Grier, former justice of the United States Supreme Court, died in 1926 at her home at 5313 Baynton Street. In the Civil War, she served as a nurse; in the course of her duties, she met President Abraham Lincoln on several occasions. She founded the Christian and Missionary Alliance.

Cuyler Hospital medical records for two soldiers wounded by gunshots.

Nurse and Sister M. Anselm Jennings

Memorial services for thirteen Sisters of St. Joseph who served as nurses in the Civil War were held at Mount St. Joseph's Convent and College in Chestnut Hill (date unknown). At the same time in Washington, a memorial to all sisters who served in the war was unveiled.

Following an address by the college chaplain, the Reverend James J. Griffin, and other exercises in the college rotunda, wreaths were placed on the graves of each of the thirteen sisters who were buried in the convent cemetery. Prior to this, Father Griffin held the service for blessing the dead.

The main feature of the exercises in the rotunda was the placing of a laurel wreath on the head of Sister M. Anselm Jennings, at that time the only living nurse of the order in the area who served in the war.

Sister Anselm, who was eighty-five years old and was in the order for sixty-six years, told of the work that she did during the war. She was on the *Commodore*, a hospital boat stationed at Fort Monroe and Yorktown. When the boats became crowded with wounded, the Northern men were brought to Philadelphia hospitals and the Southern men to Baltimore.

Teacher and Army Nurse Maria McClelland

Naaman K. Ployd, in a September 27, 1909 *Germantown Independent Gazette* article, said that one of the most popular and heroic old-time school teachers of Germantown was Maria McClelland. She was a Maryland girl: bright, intelligent, with a well-balanced brain and a big heart filled with love toward all. "Miss Maria" was one of the early teachers in the boys' primary department of the Rittenhouse Public School, and for many years, she filled the position of principal with great distinction. She was like a mother to her boys, looking to the interest of their spiritual, as well as their temporal, wants. She taught loyalty to country and to God, and many of her scholars lived to shoulder a musket and defend the flag she loved so well.

This sainted woman went to the old Haines Street Methodist Meeting, where she instructed a big class of girls. After the meeting house became too small, she, with a number of others, started St. Stephen's Church.

She lived to see many of her pupils of both the public and Sunday schools grow up and become honorable citizens. She lived to see over seventy-five men and boys from St. Stephen's Church and Sunday school, and an equal number from the Haines Street Church say, "Here we are, Father Abraham." She lived to see their vacant places filled by loyal mothers and daughters, while their boys were bleeding on the battlefields or starving in Rebel prisons.

Miss Maria McClelland left all that was near and dear to her in Germantown and became a volunteer nurse in the Union army and ministered nobly to the wounded and dying soldiers. She, like Mrs. Livermore, Clara Barton, Fanny Ricketts, Mrs. Husband, Mrs. Wittenmeyer, Hetty Jones, Mrs. Harris, Clarissa Jones (nee Dye) and hundreds of other devoted heroines, served their country well.

When there were no more suffering and no more wounded for which to care, Miss Maria found other fields to labor in. On October 13, 1883, in a Western cemetery, in the presence of a multitude of people, a casket was lowered in the ground. It contained the body of Miss Maria McClelland, the girl from Maryland, the heroine, devoted teacher and benefactor from historic Germantown.

Hospital Aide Rebecca Perot

During the Civil War, Rebecca Perot was one of the aides in the Cherry Street Hospital for the care of wounded Union soldiers.

For many years after the war, she was a member of the board of managers of the Woman's Hospital of Philadelphia, the Preston Retreat and the Friends' Female Association for the Relief of the Poor with Clothing. She was also interested in many other charitable institutions.

The death of Mrs. Perot took place in April 1913 at her home on Bethlehem Pike in Chestnut Hill. Mrs. Perot was the daughter of Adam and Charlotte Siter and was born in Stafford in Chester County, Pennsylvania. Her father was a well-known flour merchant. She was survived by one son, T. Morris Perot Jr.

Nurse and Fundraiser Hannah Ann Zell

Hannah Ann Zell was born on January 17, 1820, the daughter of Thomas Zell and Hannah Ogden Zell. She was descended from Melchior Meng, who was prominent in the early history of Germantown. She attended Friends' Schools in Philadelphia as a child and completed her education in Europe. Zell devoted much of her life to charitable work in Philadelphia and in Germantown.

During the Civil War, she nursed wounded soldiers in the hospital at Broad and Cherry Streets and aided in sending supplies to the front.

She founded sixteen libraries in small towns throughout the country and, at the time of her death, she was president of the Germantown Library and Historical Society that she had organized in 1864. She was a director for the School of Industrial Art. Zell was also the vice president of the Germantown Site and Relic Society and a member of the Welcome Society.

Hannah Ann Zell died on January 28, 1911, of pneumonia at the age of ninety-one at her home at 724 Locust Avenue; she was buried at Merion Meeting. She was survived by nineteen nieces and nephews.

Letters to Hannah Zell:

Headquarters Cairo Relief Association
Cairo June 15, 1864

Dear Madam
    I have today received your check for one hundred dollars for the relief of the Southern refugees arriving here—I have handed it to the Treasurer of our Association, whose receipt I enclose. All the packages of clothing forwarded by you have been received, and most of the articles

MISCELLANEOUS CONTRIBUTIONS.*

Mrs. James Aertsen, 6 linen shirts and old linen and muslin.

Miss Esther Aertsen, 17 towels, 9 handkerchiefs.

Miss Adele Biddle, 10 packages hospital cards.

Mrs. E. H. Butler, 6 bottles currant shrub, 2 do. jelly, 6 do. raspberry vinegar.

Mrs. Robert B. Cabeen, 3 pieces of binding for slippers.

Mrs. H. L. Carson, 43 numbers Living Age, 7 Atlantic Monthly, 18 Harper, 9 miscellaneous.

Mr. C. L. Eberle, 30 pounds castile soap.

Mrs. Cowperthwait, old muslin and linen.

Mrs Chancellor, old linen.

Miss Fewett, 13 linen towels, shreds for shoddy, old muslin.

Mrs A. W. Green, 12 Harper's Magazines, old muslin.

Mrs. Henry, 3 flannel shirts, 2 muslin do., 1 pair suspenders.

Mrs. T. C. Henry, 1 shirt, 1 pair of drawers, old muslin.

Mrs. Henderson, 5 pr. of stockings, 1 pr. of mittens, old muslin.

Mrs. S. S. Keyser, 14 bandages.

Miss Lamdin, 4 pairs of stockings, 9 pairs of mittens, old muslin and linen.

Miss R. W. Morris, 1 pr. mits, 5 magazines, 2 books, old linen.

Mrs. B. W. Morris, 3 jans of tomato soy.

Mrs. Thomas Mellor, Miscellaneous magazines.

Mrs. Mitchell, 1 linen shirt, 5 numbers Living Age, 5 Blackwood, 5 Godey, 2 linen shirts, 6 numbers Chambers', 4 Arthur's, 4 Peterson's, 7 Miscellaneous.

Mrs. H. P. McKean, 4 sheets, 4 spreads, 12 linen pillow-cases.

Mrs. Joseph Parker, old linen.

Mrs. John Rodney, 4 packages farina, 4 do. corn starch, 1 barley, 2 cocoa, old linen, 1 package nutmegs, 2 bottles whiskey, 3 pounds white sugar.

Mrs. C. Saddler, 1 pound of lint.

Miss Stevenson, 7 pair of socks, old linen.

Mrs. Stevens, 50 pairs of slippers.

Mrs. Steever, 38 yards of calico.

Mrs. Schwab, 1 dozen woolen helmets.

Mrs. Geo. W Toland, 1 pair of socks, 6 half worn shirts.

Miss Anne Waln, 2 pairs of socks, 18 handkerchiefs.

Miss Sarah Smith, 1 pair of socks.

Mrs. M. A. Wright, newspapers.

Mrs. Wm. Wister, cotton flannel, carpet for slippers, 2 books, 4 jars of pickles, 1 pair of hose.

Mrs. O. J. Wister, 15 Cornhill Magazine, 30 Athenæums, 5 pamphlets, 48 American Whig Review, 1 Journal of Arts and Sciences.

---

* For the contributions of the former six months see the Semi-Annual Report.

Contributions of clothing, food and other goods were made to the Germantown Field Hospital Association, organized in July 1863. Its secretary was Hannah Ann Zell.

Mrs. R. F. Warner, 43 Atlantic Monthly, 66 Harper's Magazine.
Mrs. A. K. Wright, 50 religious books and tracts.
Misses Zell, 14 miscellaneous pamphlets, package of papers.
Mrs. S. D. Wharton, miscellaneous pamphlets, old muslin and
    linen.

Articles made by the Association.

Mittens	8	Socks, prs	36
Arm Shields	42	Sheets	191
Arm Slings	115	Pillows	441
Bandages	219	Pillow cases	315
Drawers	319	Slippers, prs	32
Handkerchiefs	262	Wrappers	18
Pads and Cushions	604	Shirts	480
Towels	857	Chemises	109
Dresses, large and small	31	Saques	7
Skirts	66	Comfortables quilted	5
Spreads	8		
Total			4165

*Articles sent Sanitary and Christian Commissions and Field
Hospitals.*

Bandages	486	Thier's Napoleon	6
Buckets, tin	6	Miscellaneous pamphlets	61
Candles, pounds	4	Farina	128
Candlesticks	6	Handkerchiefs	712
Corn Starch	97	Lead Pencils	192
Cups	28	Lemons	186
Concentrated Milk, cans	24	Mosquito Nettings, yds	96
Coffee Pots	5	Pillows, Pads and Cushions	954
Drawers	551	Pillow Cases	319
Eye Shades	6	Pantaloons	8
Fans	73	Sheets	275
Sponges	60	Shirts	775
Socks	127	Slippers	89
Soap, pounds	44	Syrups, lemon, strawberry	
Nutmegs, pounds	2	raspberry, &c	212
Rice Flour	3	Sugar	35
Broma	2	Sago	1
Wine, bottles	27	Towels	1213
Wrappers	39	Tapioca, pounds	18
Currant Jelly	34	Whiskey, bottles	37
Slings	120	Wringer Clothes	2
Knit Helmets	14	Flannel Bands	3
Lint, pounds	9	Suspenders	16
Flour, pounds	1	Comfortables and Spreads	22
Athenæums, Nos	30	Yarn for darning, lbs	1
Atlantic Monthly, Nos	68	Mittens	27
Harper's	134	Sweet Potatoes, bbls	5
Living Age	93		

Hannah Ann Zell, nurse and fundraiser.

A letter to Hannah Zell included this drawing.

already distributed. Without speaking individually, I think I may say that the clothing sent by your Assn. has been more than ordinarily useful to us—all the articles having been new, strong, and made with great judgment. The ladies engaged in our work here beg me specially to thank you for all the great assistance you have rendered therein. We know that if it should be in your power to help us again in this way, you will not forget us. Meanwhile we pray for a great blessing upon your present noble work.

Very resp[ectfull]*y and truly yours*
[Rev.] *Thomas Lyle*

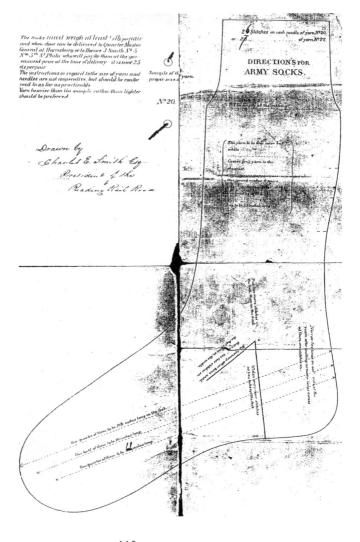

This pattern for army socks was drawn by Charles E. Smith.

U.S. Sanitary Commission, Women's Penna. Branch, 1307 Chestnut Street, Phila.,
>*April 11, 1865*
>*Richmond is Ours!!!!*
>*Lee has Surrendered!!!!*
>*Dear Miss Zell—The bale from the F.H.A.* [Field Hospital Association] *came to us at last! There seemed to be a fatality in our receiving your splendid supplies on Monday. But we did open the bale and we did enjoy every thing it contained. The comfort bags from the children (28 in number) are loved, and will be a real comfort to just so many wounded Soldiers. I saw them all packed in a box which contained 500 to go to the front today—also your shirts, towels, pillow cases, hdkfs, caps (we want more of those) and old muslin. You work splendidly, only think of 90 doz. bandages! How tired somebody's arms must have been! I can tear and ravel, but cannot wind! Mrs. Etting was not at the rooms yesterday, she is an invalid.*
>*Your friend truly*
>*Sophia W. Plitt*

MRS. SARAH KEPHART

Dedicated to the War Effort

A life-sized portrait of Sarah Kephart was presented to Ellis Post Six, GAR, by her two sons, Sylvanus and William Kephart, who are both members of that organization. The portrait was made from a small photograph that is the only picture of the famous woman in existence.

Mrs. Kephart was born in 1809, near George's Hill, which is now a part of Fairmount Park. Her maiden name was Sarah Bainbridge, and she was a relative of the late Commodore Bainbridge, who was noted for his many naval exploits. At the age of twenty-one, she became the wife of William Kephart, who was then a prosperous farmer at Penn and Germantown Avenues and who died in 1856. At his death, there remained his widow and five sons, William, Sylvanus, Alfred, John and Charles; the youngest was only nine years of age. The widow kept her family intact until the outbreak of the war of the rebellion, when the two elder sons, William and Sylvanus, responded to President Lincoln's call for troops and enrolled their names with Captain Frank Achuff's company, in the 106th Regiment Pennsylvania Volunteers, which was commanded by Colonel Turner G. Moorehead.

The five sons of Sarah Kephart served in the Civil War.

Corporal Sylvanus Kephart.

Shortly after, two other sons, John and Charles, enlisted in the 150th Regiment, known as the Bucktail Regiment, commanded by Colonel Langhorne Wister, leaving the youngest son at home until, when only sixteen years old, he followed in the footsteps of his elder brother and joined the 214th Regiment, commanded by Colonel David B. McKibbin. Mrs. Kephart then famously said that if she had five more sons, she would most willingly give them to her country's service.

All but Sylvanus and William died either from wounds received in battle or disease contracted in camp. Mrs. Kephart lived to be eighty-eight years of age, and at her death, she was buried in St. Stephen's Churchyard.

CHAPTER 6

Clarissa Jones Dye

Clarissa F. Jones was born about 1833, the daughter of Thomas and Lydia Jones of Philadelphia. She was a school teacher, and during the Civil War, she was the principal of the Rittenhouse Grammar School for Girls on West Rittenhouse Street in Germantown. In the first winter of the Civil War, she went as a volunteer to Camp Pierrepont and taught the soldier nurses how to prepare for the sick. During the following summer, in 1862, she served as a nurse in the Lyceum Hospital at Alexandria, Virginia, treating the wounded from the Second Battle of Bull Run and Chantilly.

In July 1863, when her school vacation began, Miss Jones went to Gettysburg. She was stationed in the field hospital of the Second Division of the Union Army. The hospital had six hundred patients, of whom one hundred were captive Confederates. The conditions in Civil War battlefield hospitals were horrible. They were filthy, and there were no antiseptics. There was also a camp of wounded Confederates nearby that Miss Jones sometimes visited to give help because there were no other nurses on the site. The conditions in the Confederate camp were worse than those in the Union camp. At one point, Clarissa Jones had to read the burial service for a dead Confederate officer since no chaplain was at hand.

A Wartime New Year's Journey

By Clarissa Jones Dye, written in 1888

About December 20, 1862, I made known my intention of visiting the Army of the Potomac to the girls of the Rittenhouse Grammar School, many of whom had brothers, fathers or other relatives in the army, to whom a Christmas offering would at this particular season be a priceless boon. It must be remembered that our army had just experienced a repulse at Fredericksburg on account of the pontoons not arriving on time. I only mention this fact in passing as explaining the destitute condition of our men. The army was in need of everything, so much had been destroyed or lost during the retreat, and the commissary department had not been able to replenish the stores. In my invitation to bring packages for relatives I reminded my young friends that there were many in the army who either had no friends or were too far from them to hope for a token of goodwill, and any article, either for the hospital or for friendless men, would be very acceptable.

I found it unnecessary to urge the matter as, at the close of December 23, I had twenty barrels filled to be distributed as follows: Three containing hospital stores and luxuries for the sick at Lyceum Hospital; three barrels filled with onions, apples, potatoes and pickles, one with apples only, and one with bread, rolls and cakes, for Convalescent Camp, situated a short distance out of Alexandria, on the road to Fairfax Seminary. The

The Rittenhouse School for Girls, where Clarissa Jones Dye was principal.

remaining fourteen barrels contained packages for individual soldiers, sundry comforts for the friendless.

Four little girls of Germantown, Louisa and Annie Kephardt, Laura Maxwell, and Annie Shingle, recently held a fair, from which they realized $38.12. A part of the sum they presented to the Ladies' Aid Society of Germantown, and the rest they placed in my hands to purchase hospital stores.

Dr. Read of the Pennsylvania Reserves, expressed himself very much pleased with the portion donated to his hospitals, being destitute of everything necessary for the sick, of whom he had a large number in charge. He informed me that he had not so much as a paper of cornstarch, for which some of his patients had asked him. Fortunately I was able to supply him. I will pass over the visits paid to Alexandria. Returning to Washington, we set about the task of obtaining a pass to go by government conveyance to Acquia Creek; thence to Falmouth.

Before leaving Germantown, I was waited upon by Mr. Ployd, the father of our townsmen, Naaman and William, and Mr. Shriver, who had just returned from an ineffectual attempt to reach the army. Mr. Ployd was very anxious to go, and it was a sore disappointment to him, for one of his boys was sick in the hospital. They used every argument to induce me to give up my proposed journey, as they deemed its accomplishment impossible. Finding me determined, they bade me God speed, Mr. Ployd entrusting to my care a fife for his sick son. This fife is still in the possession of Naaman and very much prized by him.

My first visit was to the office of the secretary of war, but his private secretary refused to mention my application to his superior officer, declaring it not to be thought of. Other parties had made similar requests, supported by eminent men, but they failed even to obtain a hearing.

From one department to another I carried my petition with no better success. At noon I returned to Mr. Hergesheimer, who very kindly accompanied us to the house of the venerable Professor Bache. He, at the request of Mr. Hergesheimer, wrote a letter to someone high in authority, requesting him to use his influence in obtaining a pass for us to visit the field hospitals. This document also failed. Finally we determined in the event of our efforts in another direction being unsuccessful to apply to our chief magistrate, the lamented Lincoln.

Late in the afternoon we gained an interview with Chauncey M'Keever, assistant adjutant-general, who, either sympathizing with our mission as a whole, or moved by my friend's appeal in behalf of a brother who was wounded in the late battle, granted us the coveted lines upon the condition of our returning to Washington within five days. The pass was dated December 27, 1862.

The next concern was our baggage. The assistant adjutant-general had nothing to do with transportation, so we went to Colonel Rucker's office. We found him surrounded by officers. Upon making our business known he courteously informed us that our stores could not go on the boat the next day because it was necessary that they should be examined and they must be on the wharf before 6 p.m. It was later than that hour then. He was very kind, and I am sure he was really sorry that he could not grant us our prayer. I exhibited my book containing an account of the contents of each barrel but he shook his head and said that was the law.

From his office we went to every other office in Washington that had any connection with transportation. The same reply came from all—"You must go to Colonel Rucker." Finally, in spite of the ridicule of Mr. Hergesheimer,

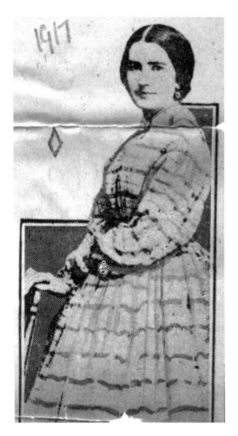

Clarissa Jones when a young woman.

we determined to appeal to General Meigs. The idea was ridiculous, come to think of it, and his dignified reception of us and the lofty tone of his reply to our request impressed us that he thought so too. "Madam, I have to do only with the transportation of the munitions of war, I am sorry I cannot aid you," he said.

Still undismayed, I determined to make one more effort. So, the following morning, leaving my companion and Mr. Hergesheimer to superintend the hauling of our barrels to the wharf, I rushed into an omnibus that was standing in front of a hotel and was quickly driven to the wharf. When my goods hove in sight I stepped up to the captain in charge and began to plead in behalf of my perishable turkeys, etc. He said, "Are you the lady who called on Colonel Rucker last evening?" I replied, "Yes, sir." "All right," he answered, "the colonel telegraphed me to pass your goods."

But the boat was moving from the wharf and my stores were still at a considerable distance, though hurrying in response to my energetic signals. The captain advised me to unload them and he would have them well cared for and guarded, and the next morning I would find them on the boat.

The very pleasant and cordial entertainment we received at the home of Mr. and Mrs. Hergesheimer forbids me to say how very much disappointed we were to be delayed even twenty-four hours. The next morning on our way down to the boat I asked Mr. Hergesheimer how I could invest some money I had remaining of the funds placed in my hands. I had intended buying some frying pans and other cooking utensils, for I remembered I had among my stores some sausage and scrapple, but Mr. Hergesheimer laughed at me saying they would find a way to cook victuals. He advised me to buy some tobacco, "for," he continued, "since the battle no sutlers [camp suppliers] have been able to reach the camp, and doing without tobacco to men accustomed to using it is a very great cross."

Accordingly, we stepped into a store, and for $3 obtained a package about the size and shape of a ream of legal cap paper. Arriving at the wharf, I took my position in line behind an officer whose luggage consisted of a tea chest. The captain demanded to know its contents. The officer whispered something—the only word that I could hear was "tobacco." "Contraband, as you know," said the captain, and, calling an orderly, he directed the tea chest to be carried into his office. It was confiscated because it was infringing sutlers' licenses. In vain the officer protested.

I think I never was more frightened. In my arms I carried this large parcel. I hastily urged my friend in front of me and vainly tried to hide the bundle with a shawl I was also carrying. She passed without question. The captain asked me what I had in my handbag. I gave it to him and called my companion to give him the key which she carries. He could feel some bottles in the bag as he squeezed it. I explained that one contained medicine for my own use and that the other held catsup. Smiling he returned the bag without opening.

We hastily made our way to the cabin and, finding a chair, I placed the tobacco upon it, covered it with my shawl and sat down upon it. I did not get over my scare till we were well on our way, my nervousness being in no wise diminished when an officer stepped up to us (we were the only ladies on board), and, excusing himself, desired to know the modus operandi of getting a pass to come on the boat. We told him we got it with no end of trouble by "women's wit." He said that he had tried so hard in behalf of a certain Mrs.—, and he had good influence at headquarters, too, but he could get no one to listen to him.

Our journey to Acquia Creek passed without further incident. Arriving there, we were politely waited upon by the officer in charge who advised us if we expected to meet friends at Falmouth to proceed at once while we had daylight. A train was just ready to start. Our stores would be forwarded as soon as this locomotive would return, there being but a single track. Each carrying what we could, a satchel apiece, the tobacco and a large wooden flour bucket filled with cranberry sauce and some pounds of butter on the top, imbedded in the mass of cranberries, we climbed upon an open truck which was already occupied by soldiers who were returning to their regiment, and by the mail carrier, who, besides the mail, had with him a haversack full of hot biscuit. Shortly after starting he opened the bag and invited us to join him in a bite. In return, we offered him some of our butter, which he gladly accepted.

Just before reaching Potomac Creek, he prepared us to enjoy our trip over it by telling us that the bridge was so shaky that he always held his breath until he was safely over it. The bridge had been burned by the rebels and this structure was put up hastily, and was very unsafe. It was not long but it was lofty. The sentinels along the creek looked like toys as we looked down.

Arriving at Brook's Station we were very glad to find two of our friends whom we were expecting to meet at Falmouth. They had been watching us for several days—Corporal Lane, of Company C, First Regiment, Pennsylvania Reserves, and his brother, Sam, of the Sixty-eighth. They had given us up and were about returning to their regiments, when our bonnets hove in sight.

At Falmouth my friend started out to find her brother and I, fearing my stores would not be forwarded promptly, decided to go back with the returning engine.

We reached Acquia Creek just in time. My stores were in a box car and the locomotive was on the point of pulling the train out when the officer, recognizing me, signaled for a halt and, finding the car, opened it and invited me to get in. The floor of the car was as far from the car as the top of the gentleman's head. There was neither ladder nor box and to toss me up was not possible. He was equal to the emergency. Kneeling on one knee he offered me the other as a step, and availing myself of his invitation and the aid of Corporal Lane, who had already mounted the car, I surmounted the difficulty.

By the light of his lantern I saw my barrels were together at one end, taking up nearly one half the car. There were a number of soldiers sitting on the barrels and boxes; I had a seat on the floor. While jolting along I heard one of the men say he was hungry and wished he was back with his regiment. One of my barrels was covered with canvas, and I noticed at Acquia Creek that a hole had been torn in it. I remembered packing it at school. It was the last one and we had no top for it, and that was the reason that we covered it with canvas. Among its contents was a large bologna sausage brought to me by a little girl whose father made it "expressly for Miss Jones to give to some hungry soldiers." I saw that barrel when I got into the car so I directed a soldier in that corner to feel about for it and get from it the sausage, also some bread that was stored in the same barrel. He needed no second bidding.

Both were handed out promptly, and someone having a penknife, the sausage and bread were cut into pieces or chunks and passed around in the darkness. How much it was enjoyed those men, if living, can even after the lapse of all these years, recall. I did not know the name of one of them. They were hungry, and that was all I cared to know. This luncheon, eaten in the pitch darkness as we crossed over the rickety bridge, is one of the pleasant incidents I love to think about.

At Falmouth our goods were taken in charge by the commissary to whom we donated a roast turkey and a loaf of bread as encouragement to be faithful in the discharge of the trust. Carrying a turkey we started through the woods towards the Sixty-eighth Regiment, whose commissary was expected to find lodging for us. When near the camp we halted while one of our party went in advance to see that preparations had been made for our reception.

It was a beautiful moonlight night. We placed a paper on the ground and on it carved a turkey. We stood around eating the supper with a relish. Suddenly the horse belonging to one of our party, that had been in the habit

Soldiers cooking over a campfire.

of sharing his master's rations, quietly put his head through the circle and seized our fowl and was walking away with it when discovered and obliged to give it up.

Lieutenant Colonel A.H. Reynolds, of the Scott Legion, very kindly offered his tent for our use, but as we had accepted accomodations the commissary placed at our disposal, we declined with many thanks. The tent was large; the fire, an open one, smoked; we were nearly blinded, but we cured it by fastening a bag in front and thus we made our quarters for the night habitable. The turkey was underdone and we toasted our portion of it on the point of a bayonet.

Our bed was a pile of boxes, upon which we slept soundly. Early in the morning we separated, my friend expecting to spend the day with her brother and to join me at night. There was a misunderstanding as to the situation of his regiment so I didn't see her again until my return to Falmouth.

Having obtained a wagon, we stowed our goods and commenced our train to Belle Plain. The papers of the day were filled with the growlings of impatient people who could not understand "why the army did not move." "If only they (the growlers) could go down to the front they would accomplish something!" "This masterly inactivity was past understanding!" "The generals were incompetent!" "The government would become bankrupt by the enormous expense of maintaining and army in the field doing nothing," etc. I wish those growlers could have gone down—how quickly their ardor would have cooled when they encountered those Virginia roads. They were literally running mud. Bad roads in the North could give you no conception of their utter impassibility. I did not attempt to get into the wagon. The horse floundered along knee deep, indeed sometimes I could not see light under him. The roads did not seem to have any foundations. I am told that in one of Burnside's attempts to move the army thirty-two horses were hitched to one artillery wagon, and yet it could not be moved. I was helped along by means of a rail fence and sometimes by having rails and branches laid like a corduroy for my convenience. To drag army wagons and artillery was a simple impossibility.

Whenever we could see signs of camping we halted and went into the woods. I think the first Germantown man that I found was Sergeant McDowell, Company C, 119th Regiment. He could hardly believe the evidence of his eyes when in response to our inquiry he came down to the road which at this place ran through the woods. He was the happy recipient of four packages. The other names as they appear in my note book are David Morell, 106th Regiment; Dr. James and Lieutenant Norman Ash, First Regiment; John H. Deal, musician, 114th Regiment; W. and H. Heckroth, Third Regiment; Louis Heck, 49th Regiment; Washington Shingle, 95th Regiment; Isaac Warr, 114th Regiment; Albert E. Sheets, 132nd Regiment; Lieutenant F.H. Achuff, 106th Regiment; G.W. Boisbrun, Third Regiment; J.H. Shingle, 95th Regiment; Louis and Frank Rauscher, musicians, 114th Regiment; J.J. Henk, 72nd Regiment; Charles P. Tull, First Delaware Regiment; H.W. Elvidge, 95th Regiment; Corporal C.W. Bolton, 95th Regiment; G. Reaver, 114th Regiment; Sergeant Sylvester Keyser, Second Michigan Regiment; Charles Righter, 95th Regiment; Lieutenant G.S. Anderson, 114th Regiment; Jacob and Samuel West, musicians, 114th Regiment, Henry H. Kephart, Fourth Regiment; Joseph Wunder, Third Pennsylvania Cavalry; B.F. Endy, 95th Regiment; Jacob Marple, Sixth Regiment; Naaman and William Ployd, 119th

One of the Germantown soldiers Clarissa Jones met up with was Naaman K. Ployd.

Regiment; W. Shriver, 114th Regiment; George Schriver, 119th Regiment; John R. Williams, Third Regiment; Benjamin and William Shermer, 114th Regiment; G.W. Cross, 95th Regiment. Opposite some of the names are messages sent back to the donor.

Naaman Ployd was sick in the hospital and his William brother off on picket duty. Lieutenant Anderson reported himself the most contented man in the regiment. Henry Kephart's father had been as far as Washington trying to reach him, hearing that he had been wounded. Lieutenant Achuff had been sent home. John H. Williams had gone to the Pennsylvania Reserves, and was waiting for me there.

Packages for the unfortunate members of the band [114th Regiment] who had been captured were taken by their comrades and the contents divided with the exception of the items of clothing, which I returned to their families.

The package of tobacco I carried on my arm in full view, no longer fearing confiscation. Every soldier I met, after the compliments of the day were exchanged, was greeted with the question, "Do you use tobacco?" Perhaps some, imagining me to be an agent of the society for the suppression of the vice of chewing and smoking, answered "No." If he bore false witness upon himself he was the sufferer. In all cases where an affirmative answer was received, I invited the astonished soldier to help himself. I think no part of the money expended by me brought forth a more satisfactory result than that invested in that bundle. You should have seen the expression of real joy that lighted up many of their faces when they did help themselves. My only regret was that there was not enough to supply all who were destitute.

Reaching Belle Plain late in the afternoon, I received a hearty welcome from the Boys of Company C, First Regiment, Pennsylvania Reserves, whose guest I was to be. We were old friends. We had visited them upon other occasions, once in the company with Miss Maria [McClelland] at their winter quarters at Camp Pierrepont, again at Harrison's Landing. They had been looking for me for a week and when I arrived they poured out of their tents, overwhelming me with congratulations and expressions of pleasure at seeing me again. The recollection of the cordial meeting, the friendly grasp of the hand, and the manifestation of joy evinced by those brave men who, forgetting their sufferings and discomforts, came forward with words of welcome, even now, after the lapse of many years, stirs up such pleasurable emotion as no honor in later life has ever awakened.

After delivering the packages to the men in camp, I proceeded to empty some of my barrels, being informed that my cabin could not be finished until I arrived with the chimney—the barrels. The cabin was built of logs with a canvas roof and a piece of tent for a door. This was fastened on the inside with buttons, holes being made in the lower edge of the canvas and nails used for buttons. Corporal Lane, assisted by the men of his company, had it built for my use.

The stores donated for the hospitals and for any soldiers in camp who needed them were very acceptable. I note some of them—shirts, jackets, thick hose, pillow cases, handkerchiefs, pillows, papers of corn starch, farina, cocoa, rice, bundles of linen, bags of lint, nutmegs, etc. One barrel held chickens and turkeys, and another homemade bread and cakes.

Calling upon Dr. Read I was warmly welcomed. He had no hospital stores of any kind. The New Year's dinner for his sick patients was the usual soldier's fare. He did not suppose there was a paper of corn starch between his headquarters and Washington, so you can imagine how glad he was to hear of the nature of the supplies the friends in Germantown had sent him. He willingly gave me permission to furnish the New Year's dinner to his patients.

The fire in my tent, by this time, being kindled, with the help of the soldiers, I prepared supper, which consisted of sausage, scrapple, bread, and coffee and was shared with all who would accept the invitation. The men sat on the ground, I should say floor, and I on the bunk they had prepared for me. I held a reception that evening such that the lady in the White House might have envied. The soldiers were so happy, most of them had friends whom I knew, some were entire strangers, all were welcome.

When nearly time for them to leave they asked me to sing something. This I could not do. I could not control my voice, I was so glad to be with them, so glad that I had accomplished what I had undertaken; all the worry, the anxiety and fatigue were forgotten in the great joy that filled my heart.

At tattoo they bade me good night, hoping I would enjoy a comfortable rest. I must describe my bed. It was composed of twigs of evergreen quite a foot and a half in thickness—I mean the bed—and covered with all the blankets Company C could spare. No bed could have been more inviting. A bright fire of coals warmed the cabin. A bayonet stuck in the ground answered the purpose of a candle stick. Armloads of wood were brought in and a plentiful supply of candles. I declined the guard they proposed, feeling perfectly safe with my friends, the soldiers of our grand army. I slept very soundly.

Early in the morning I lifted my cabin door and answered the pleasant greeting of the men wishing me a happy New Year. Our breakfast was as jolly as the supper of the night before. After the meal was over I walked through the camp looking in the various tents, making calls as it were.

Near noon I proceeded to prepare the dinner for the sick. To the turkey and the cranberries I was anxious to add a pudding. Among Lieutenant Achuff's packages I found a bag of raisins. These, with some rice, just answered my purpose and with a dressing composed of butter, sugar and corn starch, I flatter myself it was no mean dish. How did I cook it? The pudding bag was a pillow case of new muslin, the boiler an iron camp kettle and for my sauce I used an empty tomato can.

The boys of Company C helped carry the meal to the hospital. This was a great surprise to the inmates. I can see them now, their eyes glistening and a happy expression upon every face as their comrades raised them to sitting postures. At my former visit they all seemed depressed though very kindly bidding me welcome, and I can only compare their sudden brightening to the sun breaking through the clouds after a dark, gloomy spell of weather.

A box answered the purpose of a dining table and the meal was heartily appreciated, every man saying some words of gratitude to the girls and their parents for remembering them. So commenced the year 1863.

Much as I regretted it, my stay with the Pennsylvania Reserves was of short duration. The pass was good for but five days. Indeed, from its date it expired on the 31st, but as we did not fairly start until the 29th, I had no compunctions to staying two days later.

It had grown colder and the roads were in a much better condition though by no means good.

I bade the men good-bye, and as far back as I could see them from the wagon I recall them watching. The team being fresh, I reached the end of my journey by night fall and joined my friend. Early the next morning we started, I think about 4 o'clock, over the roughest road I ever walked. It was up and down ravines, over creeks, jumping from stone to stone. We had several miles to pass over before reaching Falmouth, and this cut across country could only be traveled on foot. At Falmouth the commissary very thoughtfully treated us to a tin can of hot coffee. The weather had changed from a drizzling cold morning to a clearer sky, but colder winds.

Whenever the cars stopped we all rose to our feet and stamped to warm them. We were on an open truck and we were almost frozen. The face of one of the passengers seemed strangely familiar to me and catching a sort of inquiring look in his eyes, his identity was established. I had not seen him for many years, He was Dr. William Cooper. He was blue with cold and sick. I gave him my mittens, as I could keep my hands warm in my shawl. We

Clarissa Dye, later in life.

passed safely over Potomac Creek with grateful feelings. Reaching Acquia Creek we took the boat and arrived in Washington in good time.

School re-opening on Monday, we returned to Philadelphia on Saturday.

A soldier who was visited by Clarissa Jones and enjoyed roast turkey she had brought with her said later that she came, "not as a man from a thousand and one Sanitary Commissions, with many promises and few performances, but with the good things near at hand." Her bond with many of the soldiers was that they were from Germantown families already known to each other. Some of the young men had sisters in Miss Jones's school—sisters who had helped pack the good things she brought with her.

After the war, Miss Jones married John H. Dye of Germantown. At the time of the Johnstown flood in 1888, she helped to organize the Women's Permanent Emergency Association of Germantown and was elected its vice president. The association was revived during the Spanish-American War and World War I. She served two terms as president of the National Association of Army Nurses of the Civil War. She chaired a committee on pensions for the army nurses and lobbied Congress to grant pensions to those women who volunteered during the war. A bill was passed in 1912 granting pensions to the surviving volunteer nurses. Her husband died in 1906, and she died in 1921 at the age of eighty-eight. She lived at 5810 Greene Street.

CHAPTER 7

After the War

FORMATION OF THE GAR AND ELLIS POST SIX

On May 17, 1866, twenty-eight Union veterans of Germantown organized a chapter of the "Boys in Blue," at the Germantown Town Hall. General Joshua T. Owen of Chestnut Hill was elected president. On November 16, 1866, the Germantown Boys in Blue associated themselves with the newly formed Grand Army of the Republic, becoming Post Six of the Department of Pennsylvania. The following were charter members: Lewis Wagner, commander; Marshall C. Hong; George W. Heston, adjutant; H. Oscar Roberts, quartermaster; John R. Waterhouse; Thomas Dutton; Casper Miller; Henry C. Boyd; Charles F. Walters; D.W. Bussinger; Oscar Bolton; William H. Gilbert; Gavin Neilson; Albert T. Toon; James E. Hewes; Albert J. Rorer; and William Logan.

In 1870, this post took the name of John S. Ellis, who was accidentally shot July 17, 1861, while standing sentinel at Cloud's Mills, Virginia. He was the first Germantown man killed in the war.

The National GAR was founded by Benjamin F. Stephenson on April 6, 1866, in Decatur, Illinois. Its organization was based partly on the traditions of Freemasonry and partly on military tradition; it was divided into departments at the state level and posts at the community level, and military-style uniforms were worn by its members. There were posts in every state in the United States and several posts overseas. The organization wielded considerable political clout nationwide. Between 1868 and 1908, no Republican was nominated to the presidency without a GAR endorsement. In

**As in 1861--so in 1919--
We pledge allegiance to thee "Our Flag"**

Memorial Services of Ellis Post, No. 6

Department of Penna., Grand Army of the Republic

May 30, 1919

Ellis Post Six (Civil War veterans) held Memorial Day services in 1919.

ROSTER

G.A.R.

PHILADELPHIA & VICINITY, 1892.

AVIL CO. LITH. PHILA.

The GAR published a roster of Civil War veterans (probably Post Six) in 1892.

Decoration Day, later
known as Memorial Day.

1868, General Order Eleven of the GAR called for May 30 to be designated as a day of memorial for Union veterans; originally called "Decoration Day," this later evolved into the U.S. national Memorial Day holiday.

The GAR was also active in pension legislation, establishing retirement homes for soldiers, and many other areas that concerned Union veterans. The influence of the GAR led to the creation of the Old Soldiers' Homes of the late nineteenth century, which evolved into the current United States Department of Veterans Affairs. The GAR created the Sons of Union Veterans of the Civil War (SUVCW) in 1881 to ensure the preservation of their own mission after Union war veterans had all died.

The GAR also generated several auxiliary organizations such as the National Women's Relief Corps, Ladies of the GAR and Daughters of

Above: The Ellis Post Band was composed of sons and grandsons of Civil War soldiers.

Right: Samuel Keyser Wolf was described as "the Infant Drummer of Ellis Post, no. 6, G.A.R."

Ellis Camp Nine, Sons of Union Veterans of the Civil War (SUVCW), parade at
Germantown and Chelten Avenues in 1956.

Union Veterans of the Civil War, 1861–1865, many of which are still active.
There was some controversy over the fact that the membership badge of the
GAR closely resembled the Army's version of the Medal of Honor, causing
confusion and animosity among veterans. The issue was resolved with a
redesign of the latter in 1896. The GAR reached its largest enrollment in
1890, with 490,000 members. It held an annual "National Encampment"
from 1866 to 1949. In 1956, after the death of the last member, Albert
Woolson, the GAR was formally dissolved. Its records went to the Library
of Congress, Washington, D.C., and its badges, flags and official seal went
to the Smithsonian Institution.

For many years, Post Six met in the old Germantown Town Hall at
Germantown Avenue and Haines Street. Later they met at the Engle
Building at Germantown Avenue and Harvey Street and then at 5859
Germantown Avenue.

SUVCW members at town hall on Memorial Day 1956.

THE MILITARY ORDER OF THE LOYAL LEGION OF THE UNITED STATES (MOLLUS)

On April 15, 1865, the day after the assassination of President Lincoln, three men met in the office of Thomas Ellwood Zell on Sixth Street in Philadelphia: Thomas Zell, Samuel Brown Wylie Mitchell and Peter Dirck Keyser, all residents of Germantown, where they decided to form an honor guard for the body of President Lincoln.

After the funeral, the three men decided that they would form a fraternal organization from this honor guard. A mass meeting of Philadelphia veterans was held on April 20, 1865, to pledge renewed allegiance to the Union and to plan for participation in the funeral arrangements for the president. The Philadelphia officers met again after the funeral was over to establish a permanent organization of officers and former officers patterned after the Society of Cincinnati established after the Revolutionary War. This fraternal organization became MOLLUS, the Military Order of the Loyal Legion of the United States, a hereditary organization of the officers of the union army and their descendants. MOLLUS still exists and is headquartered in the Union League building on South Broad Street in Philadelphia.

Some well-known members were General William T. Sherman; lieutenant generals Philip H. Sheridan, Nelson A. Miles and John M. Schofield; major generals Winfield Scott Hancock, George B. McClellan, Rutherford B. Hayes, George Armstrong Custer, David McMurtrie Gregg and Grenville M. Dodge; Admiral David G. Farragut; and rear admirals Bancroft Gherardi and George W. Mellville. MOLLUS members (known as Companions) included Ulysses S. Grant, Rutherford B. Hayes, Chester A. Arthur, Benjamin Harrison and William McKinley, all of whom served as presidents of the United States.

The founders of MOLLUS (all of whom were residents of Germantown) were:

(1) Samuel Brown Wylie Mitchell, A.M., M.D., has the distinction of being the owner of Insignia Number One of the Military Order of the Loyal Legion of the United States. He entered the Eighteenth Pennsylvania Volunteer Infantry on April 24, 1861, where he served until August 6, 1861. On August 17, 1861, he became surgeon of the Eighth Pennsylvania Cavalry. On December 23, 1862, he was commissioned surgeon in chief of the Second Brigade, First Cavalry Division, Army of the Potomac. On August 6, 1863, he became surgeon in charge of the Cavalry Corps Hospital of the Army of the Potomac. He was mustered out with the rank of lieutenant colonel.

Dr. Mitchell was born on August 16, 1828, and was the son of Archibald Mitchell, who for a long period was the principal of the University Academy (later the University of Pennsylvania). Mitchell graduated at Central High School in 1849, entered the sophomore class of the University of Pennsylvania and received a bachelor of arts degree in 1852. He entered the Department of Medicine while still a student in the Department of Arts and graduated in medicine in 1854. For a time he was resident physician at the Blockley Almshouse (later Philadelphia General Hospital), and shortly thereafter he entered private practice and continued until the outbreak of the Civil War.

Upon returning from the war, Dr. Mitchell came back to Philadelphia. He did not resume medical practice but gave his time to numerous societies with which he was connected. He was a founder of the Phi Kappa Sigma fraternity and recorder of the Pennsylvania Commandery of MOLLUS from the beginning of the order. He was buried in the Chestnut Hill Methodist Church burial ground.

(2) Thomas Ellwood Zell, of 723 Church Lane, died at his winter home, Zellwood, near Jacksonville, Florida, in 1905. Zell, who was seventy-seven years old, was formerly prominent in the publishing business in Philadelphia. He was a lieutenant colonel in the 101st Regiment, Pennsylvania Volunteers during the Civil War and took a prominent part in organizing the Loyal Legion (MOLLUS). After his retirement from business, his time was divided between his winter home in Florida and his home in Germantown. He was survived by his wife and a sister, Miss Hannah Ann Zell, eighty-five years old, who lived at 724 Locust Avenue.

(3) During the war, Peter Keyser served as captain of the Ninety-first Regiment, Pennsylvania Volunteers, until August 15, 1862, when he was honorably discharged on a surgeon's certificate. He had been injured at Fair Oaks from which, with camp fever, he was compelled to resign. He later was acting assistant surgeon of the U.S. Army from June 18, 1864, to March 9, 1865.

Dr. Keyser was born on February 8, 1835, in Philadelphia, of an old Germantown family who had settled there in 1688. Dr. Keyser was graduated from Delaware College, with the degrees of A.B. and A.M. He then studied chemistry for two years with Dr. F.A. Genth, of Philadelphia, during which time he published several papers in the *American Journal of Sciences*, which were later incorporated in *Dana's Mineralogy*. He then went to Germany, where he continued his professional studies until 1858, when he returned to the United States. He then entered the Medical Department of the University of Munich and later at Jena, receiving in 1864 his medical degree. On his return, he was detailed to the Cuyler Hospital in Germantown. In 1865, he filled the position of surgeon in charge of the Philadelphia Eye and Ear Hospital, which he had founded in 1864. He is credited with having given the first regular course of clinical lectures on ophthalmology ever given in Philadelphia. He was ophthalmic surgeon of the medical department of the Philadelphia German Society in 1870.

For more than twenty years, he was surgeon to the Wills Eye Hospital. In 1889, Philadelphia's mayor Fitler appointed him a member of the board of health, which position he continued to hold until his death in Norton, Connecticut, on October 1, 1908. He was buried in the old Dunkard Cemetery in Germantown (The Church of the Brethren).

Other Germantown veterans who were members of the Military Order of the United States (Insignia number in parentheses) were Alexander Biddle (6248) Twenty-first Pennsylvania; George Burnap (8388) U.S. Navy; and Emlen Carpenter (3398) Sixth Pennsylvania Cavalry.

THE MONUMENT ON MARKET SQUARE

(See also the entry for General Louis Wagner)

The monument stands in the middle of Market Square, fronting Main Street (Germantown Avenue). Artistically, it is considered one of the best of the soldiers' monuments erected. The project for its erection was originated by Ellis Post Six, GAR, of Germantown, in April 1881.

The monument is made of Westerly granite from New England, except for the capstone, which was quarried in the Wheat Field on the battlefield. Four polished granite pillars ornament the corners of the pedestal, and panels of polished granite, relieved by borderings of rough finish, bear inscriptions and bronzes.

Immediately surmounting the pedestal is the cap stone, from Gettysburg (Devil's Den), in which is set a box containing the names of 197 soldiers and sailors of Germantown who lost their lives in the war; directly above this stands the granite figure, nine feet six inches high, of an infantry soldier standing at "parade rest."

Market Square with the Civil War monument circa 1890, from a glass negative.

The monument is surrounded by a railing made of musket barrels with fixed bayonets, captured from the Rebels during the war. The four corner posts are made from a cannon captured from the British during the Revolution, and at each corner of the base of the monument stands a mortar, purchased from the United States government.

Within the enclosure on one side lies a broken cannon from the wreck of the British frigate *Augusta*, sunk in the Delaware during the War of 1812 by a shot from Red Bank, N.J.; on the opposite side, there is a pyramid of twenty-two cannon balls from the same source. There is also a shell, one of those presented to the Confederacy, by Trenholm & Co. of London and captured by General McCook at Charleston in 1865.

There was a strong movement beginning in 1947 to remove the monument, either to Vernon Park or to the campus of Germantown High School, by many local organizations, including the Germantown Historical Society. The president of the Germantown Historical Society, Leighton Stradley, wanted a type of "Colonial Williamsburg" to be erected in the area. Ellis Camp Nine, Sons of the Union Veterans of the Civil War, opposed the moving of the monument. The attempt finally failed and was abandoned around 1972.

Appendix A

OTHER GERMANTOWNERS WHO SERVED IN THE 150TH PENNSYLVANIA REGIMENT

Matthew Albert, Frederick Aucott, Edward Austin, Henry Avery, William Baker, Samuel Barnes, John Baum, Henry C. Boyd, Thomas P. Boyes, Thomas Brannan, James Brown, William Buchanan, George Campbell, John Quincy Carpenter, Henry Chancellor Jr., Joseph Chatborne, Frank Clark, John J. Collom, Newbern W. Cook, William Craig, John H. Daniels, Abraham Dannenhower, Joseph F. Darborrow, John Dedier, Isaiah Deweese, Edward Dice, William Diggle, George A. Dixon, G. Donnelly, John Doran, George Dunckley, Edward Eastburn, Frederick Eckler, Frank H. Elvidge, Herbert Elvidge, Edward Evans, Matthew Evans, Joseph Farmer, Richard Farrell, Christian Fisher, Harvey Fisher, James Fitzpatrick, Folwell James, Charles Fowler, Joseph Fowler, Isaac Fox, John W. Frame, Mellville Freas, Christian Freise, Joseph Fullmore, George Gantz, William Gerhart, John Gore, Bernard Gorman, Charles Grant, George Grantz, William Gray, Charles Greenwald, William Grindrod, Jonathan Hall, Elwood Hallowell, Philip Hammer, Edwin J. Harmer, Stephen P. Harmer, Thomas Harmer, Charles P. Haupt, John Hausman, John Hera, Abram Hill, Paul Hoffman, John Holmes, Harry Howe, Stephen Hubbard, Joseph Jordan, James Keen, Joseph Keen, Charles Kephart, John Kephart, Jacob Keyser, Samuel Keyser, William Kolb, Albert Kooker, Daniel L. Kruger, Philip Lambing, James A. Laughlin, Henry Laut, Alfred Lees, Charles Lehman, Tobias Lister, Jesse Lovett, William Lovett, Henry Lowther, James Mackey, Charles Maguire, Thomas Maguire, Isaac

R. Martindell, James Mawharter, Joseph Maxwell, James McCann, John McClellan, Thomas McCoombs, John McDevitt, John McGonigle, Albert Meeley, Jacob Meyers, William Miller, James Milligan, Enos Mininger, John N. Mitchell, Thomas Montieth, James H. Moore, William S. Moore, Harvey Morris, Patrick Mulhatton, Edward Napple, William Nitterhour, Charles Nuneviller, Henry N. Nuneviller, Terrence O'Conner, James O'Farrell, Hugh O'Neill, John O'Neill, George W. Ottinger, Thomas Ottinger, Nathan Palmer, Robert E. Patton, Epraim Paul, John Piffer, George Pollard, Reading R. Porter, John Provest, Elvin Stewart Reaver, Conrad Redefer, Jesse Rex, Samuel Rice, Henry Rittenhouse, Henry J. Rodbard, William Rodearmel, Alfred Rorer, George Sauter, George Schaeffer, Joseph Schlosser, Joseph Sharp, Harvey Sharpless, Michael Sheehan, George Shingle, James Shourds, John F. Shourds, Joseph Shourds, Reuben Shriver, Richard Sleatter, Joseph Sliffer, August B. Stadelman, Edward Steere, Samuel Stintsman, Leonidas Stroup, George Styer, Patrick Sullivan, John Swint, William Taylor, Israel Thomas, George H. Thomlinson, Gabriel B. Thompson, G.H. Tomlinson, Benjamin F. Topham, Cincinnatus Topham, Ezra Tyson, Jesse Vanartsdalen, Lewis Vogel, Jacob Wartenby, Samuel White, William Williams, James Wilson, Jonathan Wood, Joseph Worrell, Felix Wuishing, Charles S. Yocum and John Young.

Frank H. Elvidge of the Bucktails.

Lieutenant Harvey Fisher.

Private Charles Lehman.

OTHER GERMANTOWNERS WHO SERVED IN THE 114ᵀᴴ PENNSYLVANIA REGIMENT

Edward Bourgoyne, Oscar Bramon, Eli S. Bunner, John Bussinger, J. Butterworth, William Buzzard, Edward H. Campion, Isaac Clayton, William F. Clemens, Elijah Clifford, William Colbridge, Benjamin Davis, J.H. Deal, J. Dehaven, William Dimmock, Thomas Dutton Sr., Frank A. Elliott, William Fowler, David Fox, Isaac Fox, George W. Freas, Charles Gentry, John Gretzinger, Peter Harrington, James W. Haslam, John Haslam, Jacob R. Howe, Bernard Hulseman, William Jungkurth, Michael Kane, Joseph P. Kitchen, Robert Kretchmar, Daniel S. Lennen, John Lewis, George Llewellyn, Samuel Loeb, A.W. Mather, Salvador Maxwell, Samuel McCool, Louis Rauscher, George Reaver, John Rippe, Charles A. Robinson, Robert Ryley, Thomas Senatz, William Shriver, Henry S. Strouse, Charles A.Taylor, William H. Tyson, George Walker, Isaac Warr, John R. Waterhouse, Jacob M. West, Samuel West, George J. Wolf, Zachariah Wood and James Yocum.

Private Oscar Braman.

OTHER KNOWN UNITS HAVING A LARGE GERMANTOWN CONTINGENT

95th Pennsylvania Regiment, 106th Pennsylvania Regiment, 109th Pennsylvania Regiment, 118th Pennsylvania Regiment, 119th Pennsylvania Regiment, 3rd Pennsylvania Cavalry, 5th Pennsylvania Cavalry, 6th Pennsylvania Cavalry and the 15th Pennsylvania Cavalry.

Appendix B

CEMETERIES

Germantown Civil War veterans are buried in at least forty-nine cemeteries throughout the country. The known cemeteries in the Philadelphia area (and the number of veterans buried there) are:

Ivy Hill Cemetery, 750

Chelten Hills Cemetery, 78

Chelten Hills Cemetery.

Hood Cemetery, 62
Market Square Burial Ground, 40
St. Michael's Lutheran Burial Ground, 38
Trinity Lutheran Burial Ground, 35
Saint Luke's Episcopal Burial Ground, 30
Northwood Cemetery, 22
Chestnut Hill Baptist Burial Ground, 14
West Laurel Hill Cemetery, 14
Milestown Cemetery, Cheltenham, 12
Germantown Upper Burial Ground, 4
United Brethren Burial Ground, 3
Mennonite Meeting Burial Ground, 2
Philadelphia National Cemetery, unknown number

Index

About the Author

Eugene Glenn Stackhouse and his wife moved to East Germantown in 1980, but they began their research into Germantown history long before then. They joined the Germantown Historical Society in 1973, and Mr. Stackhouse was invited to join the board of the Germantown Historical Society in 1993. He served as president of the organization from 1997 to 2001.

The author has a degree in biology and worked for a biological publishing company for many years. He was also a part-time professional genealogist. He is now retired.

Mr. Stackhouse was a volunteer researcher at the historical society and began to read many of the accounts of the Civil War in the archives of the society, especially those of Naaman Keyser Ployd. Doing his own family history, he learned of ancestors and relatives who had served in the Civil War. He is a direct descendant of three Union soldiers and a collateral descendant of over two hundred Union veterans. He is a member of the Anna M. Ross Camp One, of the Sons of the Union Veterans of the Civil War (SUVCW). He and his wife live in a house in which two Civil War veterans lived and died.

Visit us at
www.historypress.net